P O C K E T S

DINOSAURS

SAUROPELTA

IGUANODON

MEGALOSAURUS
TOOTH

P O C K E T S
DINOSAURS

Written by
NEIL CLARK
and WILLIAM LINDSAY

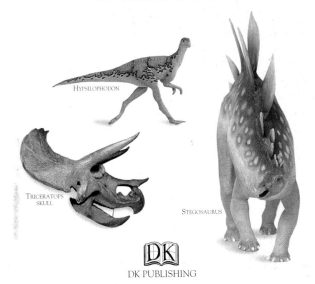

HYPSILOPHODON

TRICERATOPS
SKULL

STEGOSAURUS

DK
DK PUBLISHING

LONDON, NEW YORK,
MELBOURNE, MUNICH, and DELHI

Editor Bernadette Crowley
Art editors Ann Cannings, Sheilagh Noble
Senior editor Susan McKeever
Senior art editor Helen Senior
Picture research Caroline Brooke
Production Louise Barratt
US editor Jill Hamilton

REVISED EDITION
Project editor Steve Setford
Designer Sarah Crouch
Managing editor Linda Esposito
Managing art editor Jane Thomas
DTP designer Siu Yin Ho
Consultant Dougal Dixon
Production Erica Rosen
US editors Margaret Parrish, Christine Heilman

Second American Edition, 2003
Published in the United States by
DK Publishing, Inc., 375 Hudson Street,
New York, New York 10014

07 08 10 9 8

A Cataloging-in-Publication record for the First American Edition of this book
is available from the Library of Congress.

ISBN-13: 978-0-7894-9589-1

Color reproduction by Colourscan, Singapore
Printed and bound in Italy by L.E.G.O.

See our complete product line at
www.dk.com

CONTENTS

HOW TO USE THIS BOOK

These pages show you how to use *Pockets: Dinosaurs*. The book is divided into several different parts: two on the main groups of dinosaurs, and one on non-dinosaur reptiles. There is also an introductory section at the front, and a reference section at the back. Each new section begins with a picture page, and a guide to the contents of that section.

DINOSAUR GROUPS
The dinosaurs in the book are arranged into the two main dinosaur groups: saurischians and ornithischians. There is a separate section on non-dinosaur reptiles that swam in the sea and flew in the air at the same time.

CORNER CODING
Corners of dinosaur and reptile pages are color coded with orange, blue, and green to remind you which section you are in.

- ☐ SAURISCHIAN DINOSAURS
- ☐ ORNITHISCHIAN DINOSAURS
- ☐ REPTILES OF THE SEA AND AIR

Corner coding

Heading

Introduction

ORNITHISCHIAN DINOSAURS

CERATOPSIANS

HORNS, BONY FRILLS, and a parrotlike beak were the trade-marks of the ceratopsians. They were all quadrupedal herbivores, and many ceratopsians lived in great herds. Most ceratopsians can be divided into two groups. One group had short neck frills, the other had long neck frills. The ceratopsians were among the last dinosaurs to become extinct.

PSITTACOSAURUS SKULL

Psittacosaurus may have moved on all fours when foraging.

Caption

PSITTACOSAURUS
This dinosaur was a 6½-ft-long (2 m) bipedal ancestor of the ceratopsians. It had a parrotlike beak and a very small neck frill, but lacked the horns of ceratopsians.

Size indicator

HEADING
This describes the subject of the page. This page is about ceratopsian dinosaurs. If a subject continues over several pages, the same heading applies.

INTRODUCTION
This provides a clear, general overview of the subject, and gives key information that you need to know about it.

CAPTIONS AND ANNOTATIONS
Each illustration has a caption. Annotations, in *italics*, point out features of an illustration.

RUNNING HEADS
These remind you which section you are in. The top of the left-hand page gives the section name. The right-hand page gives the subject. This page is in the ornithischian section.

FACT BOXES
Many pages have fact boxes. These contain at-a-glance information about the subject. This fact box gives details such as the size, key features, and diet of ceratopsians.

Fact box

Running head

Annotation

REFERENCE SECTION
The reference section pages are yellow and appear at the back of the book. On these, you will find useful facts, figures, and charts. These pages introduce some well-known dinosaur hunters, along with their famous dinosaur discoveries.

LABELS
For extra clarity, some pictures have labels. They may give extra information, or identify a picture when it is not obvious from the text what it is.

INDEX
You will find an index at the back of this *Pocket*. This acts both as a species and a subject index. Every subject and type of dinosaur that is covered in the book is listed alphabetically.

INTRODUCTION TO DINOSAURS

WHAT ARE DINOSAURS?

ABOUT 225 MILLION YEARS AGO, a new group of reptiles appeared on Earth. Like all reptiles, they had waterproof, scaly skin and young that hatched from eggs. These were the dinosaurs. For the next 160 million years they ruled the Earth, before finally becoming extinct.

Powerful neck muscles were needed for ripping flesh from prey.

LAND LEGS
Dinosaurs were land animals – they could not swim or fly. All dinosaurs had four limbs, but many, such as *Tyrannosaurus rex*, walked on only their two back legs, leaving the front legs free for other tasks.

Tyrannosaurus killed prey with its strong jaws and sharp teeth.

Clawed hands

TYRANNOSAURUS REX
(LIZARD-HIPPED)

IGUANODON
(BIRD-HIPPED)

DINOSAUR DIVISIONS
Dinosaurs are divided into two groups based on the shape of their hips: saurischians (lizard-hipped) and ornithischians (bird-hipped). Saurischians had one lower hipbone pointing downward and forward, and the other downward and backward. Ornithischians had their two lower hipbones pointing downward and backward.

Period	Millions of years ago	Examples of dinosaurs from each period	
CRETACEOUS	65-145		Triceratops
JURASSIC	145-208		Stegosaurus
TRIASSIC	208-245		Herrerasaurus

TIME LINES
Dinosaurs lived through three periods in the Earth's history – Triassic, Jurassic, and Cretaceous. Different species of dinosaur lived and died throughout these three periods. Each species may have survived for only 2-3 million years.

Waterproof skin was covered in scales

Muscular tail balanced the front of the body

LIVING REPTILES
Modern reptiles, such as this iguana, have many features in common with dinosaurs, such as scaly skin and sharp claws. But many scientists believe that birds, rather than modern reptiles, are the closest living relatives of the dinosaurs.

Powerful legs

Types of dinosaur

Dinosaur designs were varied and
spectacular. A group of dinosaurs called
the sauropods were the largest land animals
that ever lived. The smallest dinosaurs
were dog-sized. Large or small, all would
have been wary of hungry meat eaters. Some
dinosaurs had armored skin for protection.
Others were fast runners
and could escape
predators by fleeing
to safer ground.

DINOSAUR TERROR
Tyrannosaurus rex and
other fierce meat
eaters had huge, sharp
teeth with which they
killed prey.

HERBIVORES
There were many more herbivores
(plant eaters) than carnivores
(meat eaters) in the dinosaur world.
A herbivore called *Stegosaurus* had
a sharp beak for cropping
leaves off plants.

ONE OF THE BIGGEST
Heavier than eight elephants and more than
80 ft (24 m) long, *Barosaurus*, a sauropod,
was one of the biggest dinosaurs.

Barosaurus' *tail
was about 43 ft
(13 m) long.*

Compsognathus
reached just below
Barosaurus's *ankle.*

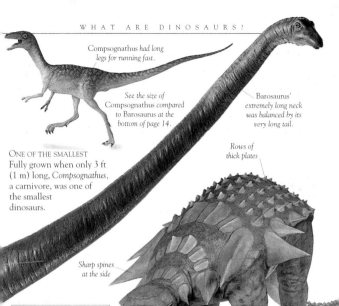

Compsognathus *had long
legs for running fast.*

*See the size of
Compsognathus compared
to Barosaurus at the
bottom of page 14.*

Barosaurus'
*extremely long neck
was balanced by its
very long tail.*

Rows of
thick plates

ONE OF THE SMALLEST
Fully grown when only 3 ft
(1 m) long, *Compsognathus*,
a carnivore, was one of
the smallest
dinosaurs.

*Sharp spines
at the side*

Thick
legs

DINOSAUR FACTS

• There were about
thirty times more
herbivores than
carnivores.

• The fastest dinosaurs
were the theropods,
which ran on two legs.

• Dinosaurs did not fly
or live in the sea.

• The sauropods were
the largest dinosaurs.

SPIKY PROTECTION
The slow-moving ankylosaurs, which were
herbivores, had armored skin for protection from
sharp-toothed carnivores. *Edmontonia* had bony
plates and spikes on its skin. It lived at the same
time and in the same places as *Tyrannosaurus
rex*, so it needed all the protection its armor could give.

More types of dinosaur

We will never know how many different kinds of dinosaur existed over the 160 million years of their existence. We do know that some fossil remains belong not to the dinosaurs but to swimming and flying relatives.

Strong plant-chewing jaws

Arms sometimes used for walking

Iguanodon was about 29½ ft (9 m) long.

Iguanodon traveled around in herds.

Long jaws

Flexible neck

A hooked claw on each hand

Baryonyx walked on two legs.

Baryonyx was about 33 ft (10 m) long.

VERY COMMON
Iguanodon was a common dinosaur. In one location, between 1878-81, coal miners in Belgium dug up more than 39 *Iguanodon* skeletons.

VERY RARE
Baryonyx is one of the rarest dinosaurs known. Only one specimen of this hook-clawed carnivore has been found so far.

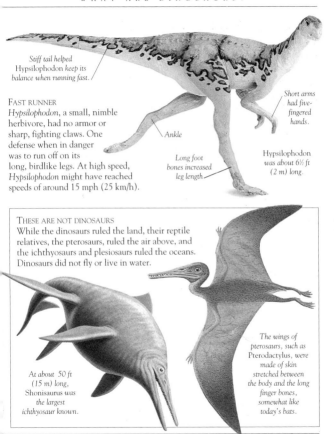

Stiff tail helped
Hypsilophodon *keep its
balance when running fast.*

Short arms
had five-
fingered
hands.

FAST RUNNER
Hypsilophodon, a small, nimble
herbivore, had no armor or
sharp, fighting claws. One
defense when in danger
was to run off on its
long, birdlike legs. At high speed,
Hypsilophodon might have reached
speeds of around 15 mph (25 km/h).

Ankle

Long foot
bones increased
leg length

Hypsilophodon
*was about 6½ ft
(2 m) long.*

THESE ARE NOT DINOSAURS
While the dinosaurs ruled the land, their reptile
relatives, the pterosaurs, ruled the air above, and
the ichthyosaurs and plesiosaurs ruled the oceans.
Dinosaurs did not fly or live in water.

The wings of
pterosaurs, such as
Pterodactylus, were
made of skin
stretched between
the body and the long
finger bones,
somewhat like
today's bats.

At about 50 ft
(15 m) long,
Shonisaurus was
the largest
ichthyosaur known.

DISCOVERING DINOSAURS

SIR RICHARD OWEN
(1804–1892)

EVERYTHING WE KNOW about dinosaurs is based on their fossilized remains. These are pieced together to make the skeletons we see in museums. Sir Richard Owen, the famous dinosaur expert, first named some reptile fossils as dinosaurs in 1841.

Fossils

Fossils are the remains of ancient living things buried and preserved in rocks. Most fossils were formed from tough body parts, such as the bones of animals or the woody parts of plants. Fossilization is a very slow process – it usually takes millions of years.

TOUGH TOOTH
Worn surfaces on fossilized teeth show how different dinosaurs ate in different ways.

SAUROPOD
EGGSHELL
FRAGMENT

IGUANODON
CALF BONE

FOSSIL EGGSHELL
Dinosaur eggshells, such as this fragment from a sauropod egg, were hard enough to be preserved as fossils.

SAUROPOD
TOOTH

OLD CONES
These pine cones from the Cretaceous period were tough enough to fossilize.

FOSSILIZED
CONES

FOSSIL BONES
Sometimes when bones fossilize, slow chemical processes capture every detail of their original inner structure and outer shape. Even when bones are cracked and crushed, it is possible to identify scars where muscles were attached.

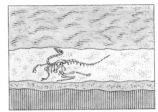

1 STORY OF A DINOSAUR FOSSIL
The dinosaur *Struthiomimus* lies dead on a riverbank. For *Struthiomimus* to have a chance of fossilization, it must be buried quickly before it rots away.

2 Buried under many layers of sediment, over millions of years, the hard parts of *Struthiomimus* change to stony fossils.

Fine bones

Fossilization occurs mainly in silt or clay underwater.

Saurischian pelvis

3 Earth movements and erosion expose the skeleton at the surface. A scientist starts to chip away the surrounding rock.

It is rare to find a perfectly preserved whole skeleton.

Long rear leg

UNCOVERED FOSSIL
An almost perfect fossil of *Struthiomimus*, lying in its death pose, has been carefully uncovered. Studying this skeleton gives scientists more clues in the dinosaur puzzle.

Preparing dinosaurs

MAKING A MOLD
To make a mold of an original bone, liquid rubber is painted on to the surface of the bone and left to set. When the rubber has set, it is removed from the bone in sections. It is then supported by cotton gauze and surrounded with a plastic jacket.

As scientists gain a better understanding of the way dinosaurs lived, museums try to arrange dinosaur skeletons in a variety of poses. Scientists at the American Museum of Natural History in New York built an exciting display. They showed a *Barosaurus* skeleton rearing up, defending its young against an attacking *Allosaurus*. Since the fossil bones of *Barosaurus* were very fragile and too heavy to display in such a pose, a lightweight replica of the skeleton was made.

POURING THE MOLD
The inside of the rubber molds are painted with liquid plastic and strengthened by sheets of fiberglass. The mold sections are then joined together to recreate the bone's shape, and are filled with plastic foam.

Pouring the plastic foam into the bone cast

Filing away the rough edges of the joins

FINISHING TOUCHES
The joins in the cast bones are smoothed by filing. The plastic bones are then painted to match the colors of the original bones.

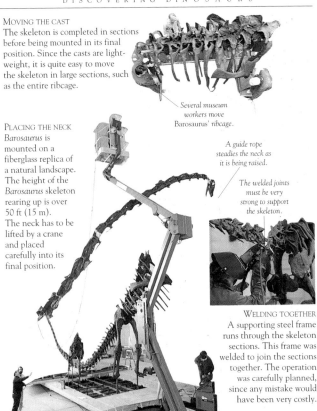

MOVING THE CAST
The skeleton is completed in sections before being mounted in its final position. Since the casts are light-weight, it is quite easy to move the skeleton in large sections, such as the entire ribcage.

Several museum workers move Barosaurus' ribcage.

PLACING THE NECK
Barosaurus is mounted on a fiberglass replica of a natural landscape. The height of the *Barosaurus* skeleton rearing up is over 50 ft (15 m). The neck has to be lifted by a crane and placed carefully into its final position.

A guide rope steadies the neck as it is being raised.

The welded joints must be very strong to support the skeleton.

WELDING TOGETHER
A supporting steel frame runs through the skeleton sections. This frame was welded to join the sections together. The operation was carefully planned, since any mistake would have been very costly.

Dinosaurs on display

The most popular feature of many museums with natural history collections are the dinosaurs. Natural history museums around the world have dinosaur displays. Scientists use these museums for storing fossils, and as laboratories for studying dinosaurs and other fossils.

STORING FOSSILS
The dinosaur fossils on display in museums are often just a fraction of the fossils the museum possesses. Sometimes thousands of fossils are housed in storerooms.

LIFE-SIZE SKELETON
Scientists and museum staff work together to construct a skeleton for display, such as this replica *Tyrannosaurus rex* skeleton. Full-size reconstructions of dinosaurs give us an impression of how they may have looked. This is particularly effective with awesome giants like *Tyrannosaurus*.

When running, Tyrannosaurus rex would have held its tail rigid for balance.

The back leg bones were thick to support Tyrannosaurus rex's enormous weight.

DINOSAUR DRAMAS
Many films and books portray dinosaurs and people as living at the same time, although dinosaurs became extinct over 60 million years before the first humans existed. Despite this inaccuracy, dinosaur films and stories make people more aware of these fascinating animals.

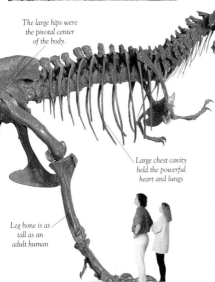

The large hips were the pivotal center of the body.

Large chest cavity held the powerful heart and lungs

Leg bone is as tall as an adult human

PREPARING A SKELETON
Fossil dinosaur bones can be fragile and are often in pieces when first collected. Scientists use special tools to remove the rock surrounding a newly excavated fossil bone. This scientist is working on a *Triceratops* skull.

DINOSAUR WORLD

THE WORLD HAS NOT always looked the way it does today. Continents are constantly moving, and this very gradually changes the appearance of the Earth. The Triassic, Jurassic, and Cretaceous worlds all looked very different from one another. Mountains grew up; erosion wore land away, and plants and animals, including the dinosaurs, appeared and disappeared.

Changing Earth

The Earth's outer layer consists of huge plates, made up of the crust (the rocky outside) and the topmost part of the mantle (the dense substance below). These plates are constantly moving, growing along one edge and being destroyed along the other.

Two plates colliding forms mountain ranges

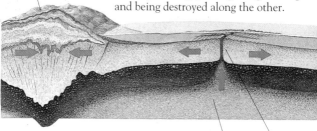

MOVING PLATES
As the plates move, they either collide, which sometimes forms mountain ranges, or they move apart, forming new crust. When plates move apart, molten mantle rock rises between them, cools, and adds to the Earth's crust.

The moving plates are lubricated by a soft layer within the mantle.

Molten mantle rock surfaces to form new crust.

Edge of plate

The constant movement of the plates is called Continental Drift.

WORLD MAP OF PLATES

PLATE BOUNDERIES

There are nine main plates and several smaller ones. The plates are in constant motion, moving at a rate of only a few inches each year.

Land was joined together

Tethys Sea

TRIASSIC WORLD

In the Triassic period, when dinosaurs first appeared on Earth, all the land was joined together forming one gigantic continent. Scientists call this supercontinent Pangaea.

Laurasia was made up of northern landmasses.

JURASSIC WORLD

In the Jurassic period, Pangaea gradually split into two continents. The continent in the north, made of large landmasses and smaller islands, is called Laurasia. The continent in the south is called Gondwanaland.

Gondwanaland

Sometimes when two plates meet one slides beneath the other.

This landmass became South America.

CRETACEOUS WORLD

Toward the end of the Cretaceous period, the continents broke up into smaller landmasses. Plates collided, forming the Rocky Mountains in North America and other mountain ranges.

Triassic world

The Triassic period was the beginning of the Mesozoic era, which lasted until the end of the Cretaceous period. The first dinosaurs appeared in the Triassic period. These dinosaurs were agile carnivores that evolved rapidly. Some became herbivores. Small mammals also appeared at this time, as did the flying reptiles, called pterosaurs.

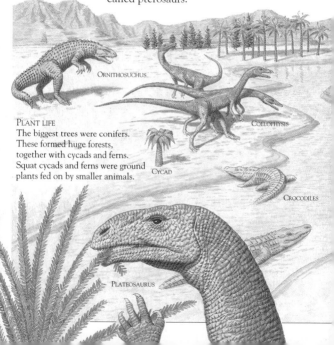

ORNITHOSUCHUS

COELOPHYSIS

PLANT LIFE
The biggest trees were conifers. These formed huge forests, together with cycads and ferns. Squat cycads and ferns were ground plants fed on by smaller animals.

CYCAD

CROCODILES

PLATEOSAURUS

LIFE IN THE AIR
The pterosaurs were cousins of
the dinosaurs, and were the
only reptiles ever to fly. They
flew above the conifer forests
catching insects. They may
also have skimmed the water
of the rivers and seas for fish.

*This pterosaur,
Preondactylus,
had a wingspan
of about
5 ft (1.5 m).*

MELANOROSAURUS

DICYNODONTS

PLATEOSAURUS

HERRERASAURUS

DINOSAUR LIFE
The number of herbivores,
such as *Plateosaurus*, increased during the
Triassic period. They were stalked by
carnivorous dinosaurs, such as *Herrerasaurus*.
Other reptiles lived alongside the dinosaurs,
such as the piglike dicynodonts.

Jurassic world

Early in the Jurassic period, the herbivorous dinosaurs were mainly prosauropods and small ornithopods. By the late Jurassic, herds of giant sauropods roamed the land. These dinosaurs, as well as other reptiles and mammals, fed on the lush plant life. The first birds appeared, but the pterosaurs remained the rulers of the skies.

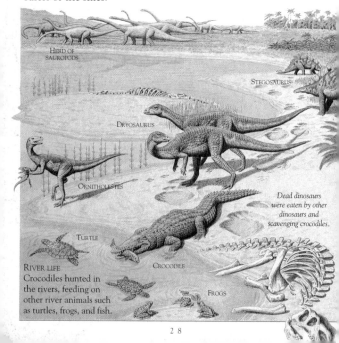

HERD OF SAUROPODS

STEGOSAURUS

DRYOSAURUS

ORNITHOLESTES

Dead dinosaurs were eaten by other dinosaurs and scavenging crocodiles.

TURTLE

CROCODILE

FROGS

RIVER LIFE
Crocodiles hunted in the rivers, feeding on other river animals such as turtles, frogs, and fish.

PLANT LIFE
Cycads, conifers, and ginkgoes
dominated the forests. Ferns and
horsetails provided a dense ground cover.

DINOSAUR LIFE
This was the age of the
giant dinosaurs. Herds of sauropods marched
across plains feeding on treetops. Fierce carnosaurs,
such as *Allosaurus*, preyed on herbivores like
Stegosaurus. Not all the dinosaurs were giants – tiny
Compsognathus also lived in this period.

Cretaceous world

In the Cretaceous period, North America, Europe, and Asia were part of a much larger continent called Laurasia. Herbivorous dinosaurs, which included the ceratopsians and the hadrosaurids, browsed among marshy lowlands. The giant sauropods became rare. In the late Cretaceous the terrifying tyrannosaurids appeared. They were the top predators until the extinction of the dinosaurs, at the end of this period.

POLACANTHUS

CROCODILE

BARYONYX

CRICKET

BEETLE

DRAGONFLY

COCKROACH

DINOSAUR LIFE
Small herbivores were more common in this period. Carnivores like *Baryonyx* may have lived on fish, while tyrannosaurids probably fed on other dinosaurs.

PLANT LIFE
The early Cretaceous landscape abounded in conifers and ginkgoes, as in Jurassic times. Later in this period, flowering plants and shrubs became common, as did trees such as oaks, maples, and walnuts.

HERD OF
HYPSILOPHODON

IGUANODON

TURTLE

*The herbivore
Iguanodon ate
leaves from conifers
and tall cycads.*

Dinosaurs today

The remains of dinosaurs have been discovered on every continent, and new dinosaur fossils are constantly being discovered. They may be found by scientists on expeditions, by amateur fossil hunters, or by accident in places like building sites and underground mines. This map of the modern world shows the locations of the major dinosaur finds.

NORTH AMERICA
Expeditions are always being organized to search for dinosaurs in North America, since rocks from the dinosaur age are exposed over vast areas. The dinosaurs discovered here include:

- *Allosaurus*
- *Triceratops*
- *Deinonychus*
- *Camarasaurus*
- *Parasaurolophus*
- *Corythosaurus*
- *Stegosaurus*
- *Apatosaurus*
- *Coelophysis*

ANTARCTICA
The climate in Antarctica was much warmer in the dinosaur age than it is today. The bones of several small Cretaceous period dinosaurs have been found here, including a relative of the small ornithopod *Hypsilophodon*.

SOUTH AMERICA
Most South American dinosaurs have been found in Argentina and Brazil. Some of the earliest known dinosaurs have been found here. The South American dinosaurs include:

- *Saltasaurus*
- *Herrerasaurus*
- *Patagosaurus*
- *Staurikosaurus*
- *Piatnitzkyosaurus*

EUROPE
It was here in the 19th century that the first dinosaur fossils were collected and recorded, and where the name "dinosaur" was first used. Dinosaurs found in Europe include:

- Hypsilophodon
- Iguanodon
- Plateosaurus
- Baryonyx
- Compsognathus
- Eustreptospondylus

ASIA
Many exciting discoveries of dinosaurs have been made in the Gobi Desert. Scientists are still making new discoveries in China and India. Dinosaurs found in Asia include:

- Velociraptor
- Oviraptor
- Protoceratops
- Tuojiangosaurus
- Mamenchisaurus
- Gallimimus

AUSTRALIA AND NEW ZEALAND
There have been many fossil finds in Australia, and one in New Zealand. There are probably many sites rich in dinosaur fossils in these countries, but they have yet to be found. Dinosaurs found in these countries include:

- Muttaburrasaurus
- Leaellynosaura
- Austrosaurus
- Rhoetosaurus
- Minmi

AFRICA
Africa is a rich source of dinosaur fossils. A site in Tanzania has held some major discoveries. Dinosaurs found in Africa include:

- Spinosaurus
- Brachiosaurus
- Barosaurus
- Massospondylus

DINOSAUR ANATOMY

THE SIZE AND SHAPE of a dinosaur's head, body, and legs help us to tell one dinosaur from another, and also tell us how the body parts were used. From the skeleton inside to the scaly skin outside, each part of a dinosaur helps build a picture of these amazing animals.

Body power

The shoulder and pelvic muscles were crucial areas of power for light, fast runners as well as slow, heavy plodders. The largest dinosaurs were not always the mightiest. Some of the smallest dinosaurs were powerful runners.

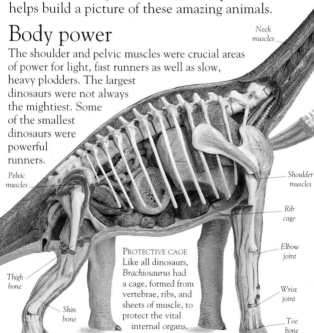

Neck muscles

Pelvic muscles

Shoulder muscles

Rib cage

Elbow joint

PROTECTIVE CAGE
Like all dinosaurs, *Brachiosaurus* had a cage, formed from vertebrae, ribs, and sheets of muscle, to protect the vital internal organs.

Thigh bone

Shin bone

Wrist joint

Toe bone

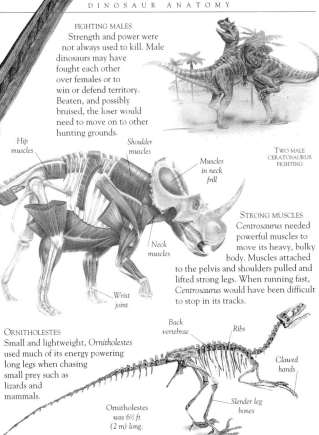

FIGHTING MALES
Strength and power were not always used to kill. Male dinosaurs may have fought each other over females or to win or defend territory. Beaten, and possibly bruised, the loser would need to move on to other hunting grounds.

TWO MALE CERATOSAURUS FIGHTING

Hip muscles

Shoulder muscles

Muscles in neck frill

Neck muscles

Wrist joint

STRONG MUSCLES
Centrosaurus needed powerful muscles to move its heavy, bulky body. Muscles attached to the pelvis and shoulders pulled and lifted strong legs. When running fast, *Centrosaurus* would have been difficult to stop in its tracks.

ORNITHOLESTES
Small and lightweight, *Ornitholestes* used much of its energy powering long legs when chasing small prey such as lizards and mammals.

Back vertebrae

Ribs

Clawed hands

Slender leg bones

Ornitholestes was 6½ ft (2 m) long.

Heads

Crests, frills, horns, and spikes adorned the heads of many dinosaurs. These decorations helped dinosaurs identify one another and were sometimes used for signaling. In a competition for territory, or control of a herd, the dinosaur with the most spectacular head might well have been the winner. Horned herbivores may have used their weapon for defense against hungry carnivores.

Large eye socket

Toothless jaws

BIRD BEAK
Gallimimus ate plants, insects, and lizards with its long, toothless beak. Its large-eyed skull looks very much like that of a big bird.

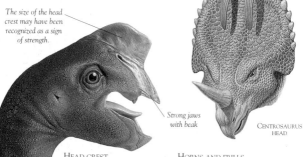

The size of the head crest may have been recognized as a sign of strength.

Strong jaws with beak

CENTROSAURUS HEAD

HEAD CREST
Oviraptor may have used their head crest to signal to one another. Although toothless, their beaked jaws may have been powerful enough to crush shellfish.

HORNS AND FRILLS
The ceratopsian group of dinosaurs had heads with a variety of frills and horns. These plant eaters probably used such decorations to frighten off attackers or to attract a mate.

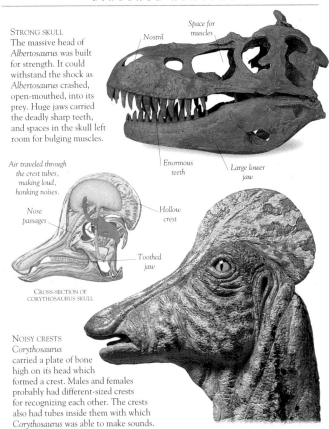

STRONG SKULL
The massive head of
Albertosaurus was built
for strength. It could
withstand the shock as
Albertosaurus crashed,
open-mouthed, into its
prey. Huge jaws carried
the deadly sharp teeth,
and spaces in the skull left
room for bulging muscles.

Nostril

Space for
muscles

Enormous
teeth

Large lower
jaw

*Air traveled through
the crest tubes,
making loud,
honking noises.*

Nose
passages

Hollow
crest

Toothed
jaw

CROSS-SECTION OF
CORYTHOSAURUS SKULL

NOISY CRESTS
Corythosaurus
carried a plate of bone
high on its head which
formed a crest. Males and females
probably had different-sized crests
for recognizing each other. The crests
also had tubes inside them with which
Corythosaurus was able to make sounds.

Necks

For dinosaurs, as with other animals, the neck was a vital channel between the head and body. Food passed from the mouth to the stomach through the neck; air was fed along the windpipe between the nostrils and lungs; nerves carried messages to and from the brain and body, and blood traveled through arteries and veins. All of these lifelines, as well as powerful muscles, were supported on the framework of neck vertebrae (neck bones).

BAROSAURUS
NECK VERTEBRA

LONG AND FLEXIBLE
Herbivorous long-necked dinosaurs like *Barosaurus* probably used their flexible necks for cropping leaves from a large area of low-lying foliage while standing still. But if they needed to, they could have reached up to the leaves in tall trees.

Muscles were attached to spines on the vertebrae

STRONG AND LIGHT
The long neck of *Diplodocus* was made up of 15 vertebrae. These bones had deep hollows inside them to make them lightweight, although they remained very strong. A notch on top of each vertebra carried a strong ligament, which supported the neck in the way that wires support a suspension bridge.

Barosaurus's neck was 30 ft (9.1 m) long.

SHORT AND STOUT
Allosaurus, a fierce and terrifying carnivore, had a short and stout neck. The neck bones were cupped tightly together to give a very mobile and curved neck. When *Allosaurus*'s jaws bit into prey, powerful neck muscles pulled the massive head up and back, tearing chunks of flesh from the victim.

Curved neck

Powerful jaws with huge, sharp teeth

LIKE AN OSTRICH
Gallimimus held its head high above its shoulders, like an ostrich. In this position, *Gallimimus* could swivel its head on its long neck to give good vision in all directions.

Long, flexible neck

The skull may have weighed as much as 113 lb (51 kg).

Very short neck

HEAD SUPPORT
Triceratops had an extension at the back of its skull made of solid bone. This made the skull very heavy. A short and very strong neck was needed to support the huge weight.

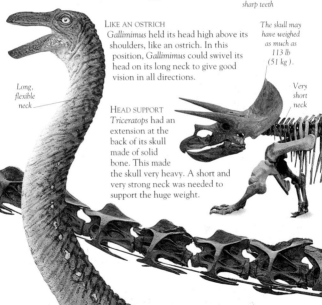

Dinosaur limbs

IGUANODON FOOT BONE

Dinosaurs held their legs directly beneath the body, unlike other reptiles, which crawl with their legs held out from the sides of the body. Huge herbivorous dinosaurs, such as *Diplodocus*, walked on all fours with front and rear legs supporting bulky bodies. Most carnivores, such as *Albertosaurus*, walked on the two back legs, leaving the front limbs free for catching and holding prey.

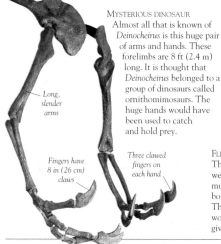

Femur (thigh bone)

Knee

Muscle

Ankle

Metatarsals

Toe

MYSTERIOUS DINOSAUR
Almost all that is known of *Deinocheirus* is this huge pair of arms and hands. These forelimbs are 8 ft (2.4 m) long. It is thought that *Deinocheirus* belonged to a group of dinosaurs called ornithomimosaurs. The huge hands would have been used to catch and hold prey.

Long, slender arms

Fingers have 8 in (26 cm) claws

Three clawed fingers on each hand

FLESH AND BONE
The rear legs of *Albertosaurus* were powered by large muscles that pulled on the bones to make them move. The ankle and metatarsals worked as part of the leg, giving a longer stride.

40

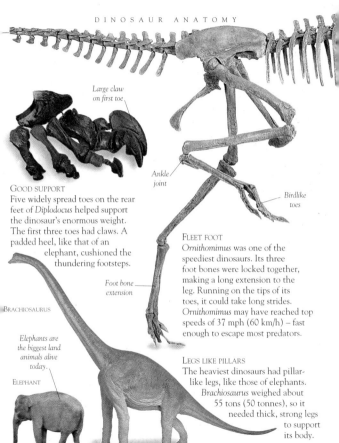

GOOD SUPPORT
Five widely spread toes on the rear
feet of *Diplodocus* helped support
the dinosaur's enormous weight.
The first three toes had claws. A
padded heel, like that of an
elephant, cushioned the
thundering footsteps.

*Large claw
on first toe*

*Ankle
joint*

*Birdlike
toes*

*Foot bone
extension*

FLEET FOOT
Ornithomimus was one of the
speediest dinosaurs. Its three
foot bones were locked together,
making a long extension to the
leg. Running on the tips of its
toes, it could take long strides.
Ornithomimus may have reached top
speeds of 37 mph (60 km/h) – fast
enough to escape most predators.

BRACHIOSAURUS

*Elephants are
the biggest land
animals alive
today.*

ELEPHANT

LEGS LIKE PILLARS
The heaviest dinosaurs had pillar-
like legs, like those of elephants.
Brachiosaurus weighed about
55 tons (50 tonnes), so it
needed thick, strong legs
to support
its body.

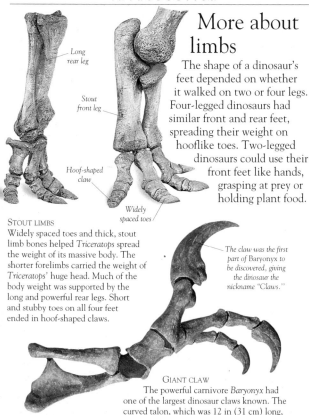

More about limbs

The shape of a dinosaur's feet depended on whether it walked on two or four legs. Four-legged dinosaurs had similar front and rear feet, spreading their weight on hooflike toes. Two-legged dinosaurs could use their front feet like hands, grasping at prey or holding plant food.

Long rear leg

Stout front leg

Hoof-shaped claw

Widely spaced toes

STOUT LIMBS
Widely spaced toes and thick, stout limb bones helped *Triceratops* spread the weight of its massive body. The shorter forelimbs carried the weight of *Triceratops'* huge head. Much of the body weight was supported by the long and powerful rear legs. Short and stubby toes on all four feet ended in hoof-shaped claws.

The claw was the first part of Baryonyx to be discovered, giving the dinosaur the nickname "Claws."

GIANT CLAW
The powerful carnivore *Baryonyx* had one of the largest dinosaur claws known. The curved talon, which was 12 in (31 cm) long, formed a huge weapon on *Baryonyx's* hand.

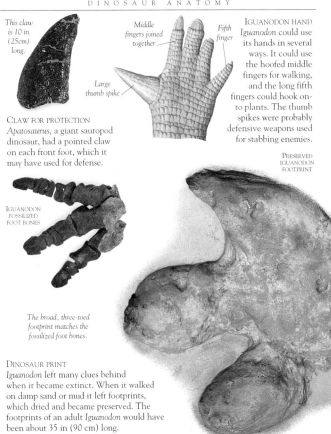

This claw is 10 in (25cm) long.

Middle fingers joined together

Fifth finger

Large thumb spike

IGUANODON HAND
Iguanodon could use its hands in several ways. It could use the hoofed middle fingers for walking, and the long fifth fingers could hook on-to plants. The thumb spikes were probably defensive weapons used for stabbing enemies.

CLAW FOR PROTECTION
Apatosaurus, a giant sauropod dinosaur, had a pointed claw on each front foot, which it may have used for defense.

PRESERVED IGUANODON FOOTPRINT

IGUANODON FOSSILIZED FOOT BONES

The broad, three-toed footprint matches the fossilized foot bones.

DINOSAUR PRINT
Iguanodon left many clues behind when it became extinct. When it walked on damp sand or mud it left footprints, which dried and became preserved. The footprints of an adult *Iguanodon* would have been about 35 in (90 cm) long.

Tails

Dinosaur tails had many
uses, and tail bones can
tell us a lot about their
owners. Flexible tails
ending with long, thin
bones were the trademark
of the giant sauropod dinosaurs.
Dinosaurs that ran on two legs had tail
bones that locked stiffly together to
help give balance. Tails ending in
lumps and spikes were used as weapons
against attacking enemies.

*Deinonychus
could run very
fast when
chasing prey.*

*Tail bones
tightly locked
together*

BALANCING ACT
Scientists once believed that
Parasaurolophus used its thick tail for
swimming by sweeping it from side to side
like a fish's tail. But they now think that the
tail counterbalanced the front of the body.

TAIL WHIP
When defending itself, *Diplodocus* used its long tail like
a huge whip to swipe at its attacker. The tail had 73
bones joined together, and made a powerful weapon
with its thin, whiplike ending.

*Tail held stiffly
behind body*

TAIL RUDDER
The tail bones of *Deinonychus* were locked together
by long bony rods, which made the tail stiff. When
Deinonychus was running or jumping, it could steer
and balance itself by moving its tail from side to side.

*Heavy
tail club*

SWINGING CLUB
Euoplocephalus' tail ended in
solid, bony lumps. Enemies risked
serious injury from a swing of
the tail club.

TAIL SPINES
Spiny *Stegosaurus* kept its
attackers at bay by swinging
its spiked tail toward their
head or soft underside.

*Spikes were
made of
bone
covered with
horn*

*Whiplike
end of tail*

Skin

Lizards and snakes, crocodiles, and turtles – all have the tough, scaly skin that is a trademark of reptiles. Dinosaurs were no exception. Their skin, preserved long enough in silt or clay to leave fossilized imprints, shows patterns of large and small bumps. Some dinosaurs, like the ankylosaurs, had spikes and scutes (plates or lumps of bone) embedded in their thick skin to give protection against attack from more dangerous dinosaurs.

SCUTE SHAPE
Bony scutes, such as this one, were inset into the skin of *Polacanthus*, an early relative of the ankylosaurs.

BONY BARRIER
Polacanthus' protective coat of horn-covered scutes was a formidable barrier against the teeth of hungry predators. The arrangement of the scutes can be seen in fossil remains of *Polacanthus*.

Fossilized scute

CROCODILE SCALES
Crocodiles have a leathery skin of lumpy scales. Like dinosaurs, they have scutes embedded in the back, which add to the skin's toughness. The skin of crocodiles and other reptiles is also waterproof, keeping body moisture in but water out.

Crocodile skin in close-up

ARMOR-PLATED
Ankylosaurs were among the most
heavily protected of all dinosaurs.
Large, platelike scutes lay side by
side along the upper part of the
body, like a suit of armor.

FOSSIL
ANKYLOSAUR
SCUTE

*Scutes were
ridged in the
middle*

SPIKES AND SCUTES
As well as scutes, the ankylosaur
Euoplocephalus had thorn-shaped
spikes across its shoulders as an
added deterrent.

*Shoulder
spike*

EUOPLOCEPHALUS

WRAPPED IN SKIN
In rare cases, a dinosaur's dead
body dried and shriveled instead
of rotting away. This *Edmontosaurus*
fossil has the skin impression preserved and
wrapped around
the skeleton.

*Small
bumps*

SKIN PATTERN
Corythosaurus had no protective
armor. Its skin, a mosaic of small,
bumpy scales, was wrinkled and
folded around the moving parts
of the body.

*This fossil is
65 million
years old.*

DINOSAUR LIFESTYLES

ALTHOUGH DINOSAURS died out
65 million years ago, we know a
lot about their lifestyles. Herbivores
and carnivores lived in the world
of dinosaurs. Some dinosaurs cared
for their young. But whether they
were warm-or cold-blooded has yet
to be established.

LIFESTYLE FACTS
• Some dinosaurs may
have lived for 200 years.
• *Carcharodontosaurus*
is the largest land-living
carnivore found to date.
• The largest dinosaur
eggs probably belonged
to the sauropod
Hypselosaurus.
• Dinosaur embryos
have been found
fossilized in their eggs.

Carnivores

Most carnivores had deadly sharp teeth
and claws. Some hunted in packs, some
hunted alone, and others may have
scavenged on dead animals which
were possibly killed
by disease.

FAST FOOD
Dromaeosaurus had
features common to many
carnivores. It was fast,
agile, and armed with
sharp teeth and claws.
Dromaeosaurus may have
hunted in packs,
chasing and
bringing down
much larger animals.

*Clawed
hands
gripped prey*

*Long,
slender
legs*

*Slashing
talon flicked
forward*

Sharp, serrated teeth lined the long jaws.

Lethal claw

BARYONYX
From the side, *Baryonyx's* skull appears crocodile shaped. *Baryonyx* may have used its long and narrow snout for catching fish.

CUTTING CLAW
Like *Dromaeosaurus*, *Deinonychus* had a lethal weapon – a 6-in-long (15 cm) curved claw on each hind foot. When *Deinonychus* caught prey, it flicked the claw forward to cut deep into its victim.

TERRIBLE TEETH
The teeth of carnivorous dinosaurs were sharp with serrated (sawlike) edges for cutting through flesh and bones.

LOWER JAW OF
ALBERTOSAURUS

MEATY DIET
Tyrannosaurus rex was one of the fiercest carnivores. With its powerful body and massive head, it overwhelmed victims, delivering a fatal, biting blow with its deadly jaws.

Small hands could tear food apart

Herbivores

Plant-eating dinosaurs had to eat large amounts of plants every day to fuel their bodies. An herbivore's special diet needed special ways of eating and digesting food. Some herbivores' teeth were shaped for chopping, raking, or crushing. Other herbivores had sharp beaks for snipping leaves and twigs. Once swallowed, these tough plants may have taken days to digest.

GRINDING GUT
Barosaurus did not chew its food – it swallowed tough leaves and twigs whole. In a part of its stomach, stones called gastroliths ground the food for digestion.

SMOOTH STONES
Gastroliths have been found near the skeletons of several dinosaurs.

HERBIVORE FACTS

• All ornithischian dinosaurs were herbivores.

• Some herbivores had up to 960 teeth.

• There were no flowers for dinosaurs to eat until about 125 million years ago.

• Herds of herbivores may have migrated during dry seasons to find fresh food supplies.

• Some of the plants the dinosaurs ate, such as pine trees, ferns, and cycads, still grow today.

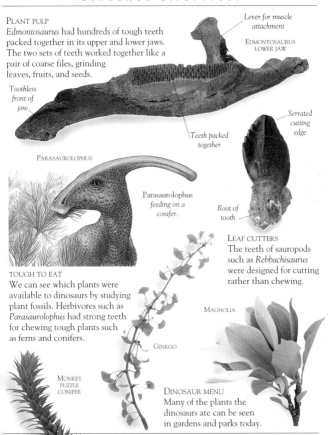

PLANT PULP

Edmontosaurus had hundreds of tough teeth packed together in its upper and lower jaws. The two sets of teeth worked together like a pair of coarse files, grinding leaves, fruits, and seeds.

Lever for muscle attachment

EDMONTOSAURUS LOWER JAW

Toothless front of jaw

Teeth packed together

PARASAUROLOPHUS

Parasaurolophus feeding on a conifer.

Serrated cutting edge

Root of tooth

LEAF CUTTERS

The teeth of sauropods such as *Rebbachisaurus* were designed for cutting rather than chewing.

TOUGH TO EAT

We can see which plants were available to dinosaurs by studying plant fossils. Herbivores such as *Parasaurolophus* had strong teeth for chewing tough plants such as ferns and conifers.

MAGNOLIA

GINKGO

MONKEY PUZZLE CONIFER

DINOSAUR MENU

Many of the plants the dinosaurs ate can be seen in gardens and parks today.

Senses

Well-developed sight, smell, and hearing were crucial to the dinosaurs' long-running success. Dinosaurs used these vital senses daily for survival in their hostile world. Dinosaurs that were active hunters tracked prey by following noises and scents. Many dinosaurs lived in groups, and protected their young by listening and watching for predators.

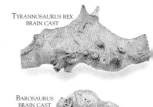

TYRANNOSAURUS REX BRAIN CAST

BAROSAURUS BRAIN CAST

BRAIN CASTS
Tyrannosaurus rex's brain was bigger than *Barosaurus*'. Brains are too soft to fossilize, but casts from the inside of dinosaur skulls show us their shapes and sizes.

CROSS-SECTION OF SKULL OF PARASAUROLOPHUS

Long air passages

SKULL OF PARASAUROLOPHUS

Crest was 3 ft (1 m) long

Teeth

Nasal opening where air enters

MAKING NOISES
Parasaurolophus and other crested dinosaurs could produce noisy signals from their head crests, identifying themselves to each other or warning of danger. Tubular sound chambers ran from the nose of *Parasaurolophus* up into its crest. Air traveled through this prehistoric "trombone," where it vibrated as sound.

COLOR

VIEW FROM LEFT

VIEW FROM RIGHT

BLACK AND WHITE

VIEW FROM LEFT

VIEW FROM RIGHT

DOUBLE VISION

We do not know if dinosaurs could see in color, but eye position affected the kind of image seen. Eyes on the sides of the head, common in herbivores, sent two different pictures to the brain.

COLOR

SINGLE VISION

Brain size is not always a sign of intelligence, but big-brained *Troodon* was probably one of the smartest dinosaurs. *Troodon* had large eyes and good vision. It benefitted from stereoscopic sight, which means it saw one image, the way that we do. Whether it could see in color or black and white, *Troodon* could judge distance when chasing or catching its prey.

BLACK AND WHITE

Warm and cold blood

Reptiles are cold-blooded, which means that they depend on conditions outside their body, such as the Sun's heat, for temperature control. Warm-blooded animals, such as mammals, produce heat from food energy, have hair for warmth, and sweat to cool down. Although dinosaurs were reptiles, much of their behavior, such as agile running, has more in common with mammals. Scientists are therefore puzzled over whether dinosaurs were warm- or cold-blooded.

Blood vessels

Blood vessels

CROSS-SECTION OF MAMMAL BONE

CROSS-SECTION OF REPTILE BONE

BLOOD AND BONES

Dinosaurs had bones more like mammals than reptiles. Mammal bones contain far more blood vessels than reptile bones.

Spinosaurus was about 40 ft (12 m) long.

Side view of plate

Cross-section of plate

STEGOSAURUS BACK PLATE FOSSILS

SAIL BACK

Spinosaurus had a large skin "sail" on its back. This could have been used to control body temperature, absorbing the Sun's warmth in the morning and, in the heat of the day, allowing the blood to cool in the breeze. *Stegosaurus* may have used its back plates in a similar way.

COLD-BLOODED SUNBATHER

A typical cold-blooded creature, such as a lizard, spends hours sunbathing to raise the body's temperature to a level where it can work effectively. To avoid overheating, the lizard can cool off in the shade. When it is cold at night, or in the winter, reptiles are inactive.

Lizard sunbathing

Velociraptor was feathered

GOOD EXAMPLE

Velociraptor is one of the best arguments for dinosaurs being warm-blooded animals. Fast-moving and agile, *Velociraptor* had a lifestyle better suited to warm-blooded killers like wolves than to reptiles like lizards.

High blood pressure was needed to reach a brain 50 ft (15 m) above the ground.

Long jaws with small, pointed teeth for catching and eating fish

BLOOD PRESSURE

Tall dinosaurs needed high blood pressure to pump blood to their brain. But down at the level of their lungs, such high pressure would be fatal. Warm-blooded animals have a twin pressure system. Perhaps dinosaurs had a similar system.

Skin "sail" was supported by spines projecting from the vertebrae

BRACHIOSAURUS

Eggs, nests, and young

Dinosaurs laid eggs, like most other reptiles as
well as birds. In recent years, scientists have
discovered dinosaur nesting sites that gave
them an insight into the early life of dinosaurs.
These sites showed that some young stayed in
their nests, cared for by adults, until they were
old enough to leave. They also showed that
dinosaurs, like many birds, used the same
nesting sites year after year.

*Fossil egg with
broken eggshell
fragments*

EGG FIND
Fossil nests found in
Mongolia in the late
1920s revealed
dinosaur eggs for the
first time. Once
believed to be from
Protoceratops, the eggs
are now known to
belong to *Oviraptor*.

*Young set
off in search
of food*

SMALL EGGS
These fossilized
sauropod eggs, which are
only 6 in (15 cm) in diameter, could have
produced young that grew to an adult length
of 39 ft (12 m). It probably took sauropods
several years to reach their adult size.

HOME LIFE

Female *Maiasaura* laid about 25 eggs in a nest that was dug in the ground and lined with leaves and twigs. Young *Maiasaura* were about 12 in (30 cm) long when they hatched. They were reared in the nest until they grew to about 5 ft (1.5 m), when they would be old enough to start fending for themselves.

FOSSILIZED MAIASAURA EGG AND SKELETON OF YOUNG

Maiasaura hatchlings were very weak.

EARLY START

Unlike the *Maiasaura* young, which were cared for by their mother for several weeks, *Troodon* young left their nests as soon they hatched. The young *Troodon* nesting sites were built on muddy islands in lakes, probably for protection from predators.

Newly hatched Troodon leaving nest

THE FIRST DINOSAURS

SEVERAL GROUPS of reptiles
existed before the dinosaurs
appeared. One group was the
thecodonts. These were the
ancestors of the dinosaurs, and
they probably also gave rise to the
pterosaurs and the crocodiles.
Thecodonts were large carnivores
that had straighter legs than other
reptiles. The first dinosaurs were
also carnivores, and the earliest
known dinosaur, *Eoraptor*, first
appeared 228 million
years ago.

A VERY EARLY DINOSAUR
Eoraptor may have been
the first dinosaur. It was
discovered in 1992 in
Argentina. *Eoraptor* had a
crocodile-like skull with
sharp, curved teeth.

*Jaws were
lined with sharp
teeth*

*Long, stiff
tail*

*Long tail acted as a
counterbalance to the
front of the body*

STAURIKOSAURUS

*Staurikosaurus
was about 6½ ft
(2 m) long.*

*Long, birdlike
back legs*

STAURIKOSAURUS
Speedy *Staurikosaurus* was one of
the first carnivorous dinosaurs. It
had long, tooth-lined jaws for
catching its prey, which it chased
on its long and slender back legs.

FIRST DINOSAURS
FACTS

• The earliest
dinosaurs have
come from Triassic
period rocks.

• Mammals were
around at the same time
as the dinosaurs.

• The earliest dinosaurs
were all carnivores.

• The first herbivores
appeared in the late
Triassic period.

HERRERASAURUS
A light and slender
skeleton made
Herrerasaurus an
agile hunter. It was
about 10 ft (3 m)
long and ate other
small reptiles.

*Scaly skin typical
of reptiles*

*Long and
narrow
head*

HERRERASAURUS

*Sharp
teeth*

EARLY CARNIVORE
Herrerasaurus lived about 230
million years ago. It had many
features in common with later
carnivorous dinosaurs, such as sharp
teeth and claws, and strong back legs.

TWO-LEGGED RUNNER
Ornithosuchus and other
thecodonts were the
ancestors of the dinosaurs of
the Jurassic and Cretaceous periods.
About 13 ft (4 m) long, it walked on
all fours, but ran on its two back legs.

ORNITHOSUCHUS

DINOSAUR EXTINCTION

AROUND 65 MILLION years ago, the dinosaurs became extinct. At the same time, other creatures, such as the sea and air reptiles, also died out. There are many theories for this extinction. But, as with so many facts about dinosaurs, no one really knows for sure what happened.

ASTEROID THEORY
At the end of the Cretaceous period a giant asteroid struck Earth. The impact resulted in a dust cloud which circled the globe, blocking out the sunlight and bringing cold, stormy weather.

Even the mighty Tyrannosaurus rex could not survive extinction.

SLOW DEATH
The dinosaurs died out gradually, perhaps over a period of several million years. *Tyrannosaurus rex* was one of the last dinosaurs to become extinct.

MAGNOLIA

FLOWERS
Flowering plants
may have contributed to the
extinction of the dinosaurs. Many
of these plants would have been
poisonous, and any herbivorous
dinosaur that ate them may have
died. Many carnivores, which fed
on herbivores, would then have
died because of lack of food.

VOLCANO THEORY
Many volcanoes were active during the
Cretaceous period. There were vast lava flows
in the area that is now India. This would have
poured huge amounts of carbon dioxide into
the air, causing overheating, acid rain,
and the destruction of
the protective
ozone layer.

*Crocodiles have not
changed much in
appearance over the years.*

Megazostrodon
*was a mammal
that lived in
the Triassic
period.*

MAMMALS
Mammals appeared
during the Triassic period,
when they lived alongside the
dinosaurs. They became the
dominant land animals after
the dinosaurs' extinction.

SURVIVING REPTILES
Crocodiles were
around before
the dinosaurs,
and are still alive today. The
reason these reptiles survived
while the dinosaurs died out
is a complete mystery.

SAURISCHIAN DINOSAURS

ABOUT SAURISCHIANS

THERE WERE two main groups of saurischians – the theropods and the sauropodomorphs. The largest dinosaurs, and some of the smallest, were saurischians. This group differed from ornithischians mainly because of the shape of the hipbones.

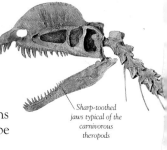

Sharp-toothed jaws typical of the carnivorous theropods

SAUROPODOMORPHS

Members of the sauropodomorph group were mainly herbivorous and quadrupedal (walked on four legs). The sauropodomorphs included the longest of all dinosaurs, *Seismosaurus*, which was about 130 ft (40 m) long.

TYRANNOSAURUS REX

BRACHIOSAURUS – A SAUROPODOMORPH

COMPSOGNATHUS

THEROPODS

All theropods were carnivores, and were bipedal (walked on two legs only). One of the smallest dinosaurs, *Compsognathus*, and the largest land-based carnivore, *Tyrannosaurus rex*, belonged in the theropod group.

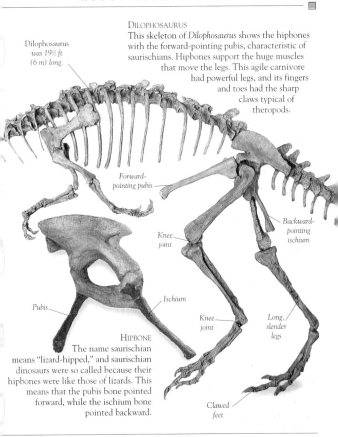

DILOPHOSAURUS
This skeleton of *Dilophosaurus* shows the hipbones with the forward-pointing pubis, characteristic of saurischians. Hipbones support the huge muscles that move the legs. This agile carnivore had powerful legs, and its fingers and toes had the sharp claws typical of theropods.

Dilophosaurus was 19½ ft (6 m) long.

Forward-pointing pubis

Knee joint

Backward-pointing ischium

Pubis

Ischium

Knee joint

Long, slender legs

HIPBONE
The name saurischian means "lizard-hipped," and saurischian dinosaurs were so called because their hipbones were like those of lizards. This means that the pubis bone pointed forward, while the ischium bone pointed backward.

Clawed feet

THEROPODS

THE GROUP of dinosaurs called the theropods were the killers of the dinosaur world. Often large and ferocious, these carnivores usually walked on their two clawed rear feet. Theropod means "beast feet," but their feet were very birdlike. Each foot had three toes for walking on, with long foot bones that added to the length of the legs. Sharp-clawed hands were often used for attacking and catching hold of prey.

EARLY THEROPOD
Dilophosaurus lived during the early part of the Jurassic period. An agile predator, it was one of the first large carnivorous dinosaurs.

Tail

FOSSIL FIND
Coelophysis hunted lizards and small dinosaurs. But in this fossilized *Coelophysis* skeleton, there are skeletons of young of the same species among the ribs, indicating that *Coelophysis* was also a cannibal.

Coelophysis was 10 ft (3 m) long.

Bones of young in ribcage

THEROPOD FACTS

• All theropods were carnivores.

• *Coelophysis* was one of the first theropods, living about 220 million years ago.

• *Tyrannosaurus rex* was one of the last theropods, living 65 million years ago.

• Many theropods had no fourth or fifth fingers.

• At least five vertebrae supported the pelvis of theropods.

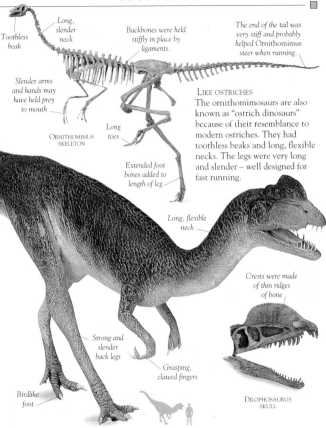

Long, slender neck

Toothless beak

Backbones were held stiffly in place by ligaments.

The end of the tail was very stiff and probably helped Ornithomimus steer when running.

Slender arms and hands may have held prey to mouth

ORNITHOMIMUS SKELETON

Long toes

Extended foot bones added to length of leg

LIKE OSTRICHES

The ornithomimosaurs are also known as "ostrich dinosaurs" because of their resemblance to modern ostriches. They had toothless beaks and long, flexible necks. The legs were very long and slender – well designed for fast running.

Long, flexible neck

Crests were made of thin ridges of bone

Strong and slender back legs

Grasping, clawed fingers

Birdlike foot

DILOPHOSAURUS SKULL

Carnosaurs

Of all the theropods, the ferocious carnosaurs are probably the most famous. Some carnosaurs could run as fast as 22 mph (35 km/h) on their large and powerful back legs. Massive heads carried a fearsome array of enormous serrated and curved teeth. *Tyrannosaurus rex* was the largest of the carnosaurs, and the most successful predator in the Cretaceous period. During the Jurassic, *Allosaurus* was the top predator.

Small first toe

ALLOSAURUS FOOT
Like all carnosaurs, *Allosaurus* walked on three large, clawed toes. The feet were strong because they had to bear the weight of the body. The first toe was small and faced backward, off the ground.

Curved neck

Long, tooth-lined jaws could open wide to swallow lumps of meat.

Large, three-fingered hands had hooked claws

Front limbs were small and weak compared to the rest of the body

Ischium

Long foot bones increased leg length

ALLOSAURUS
Complete carnosaur skeletons are a rare find. There have been many finds of *Allosaurus* parts, including more than 60 skeletons in one quarry, so a complete picture of this powerful carnivore can be created.

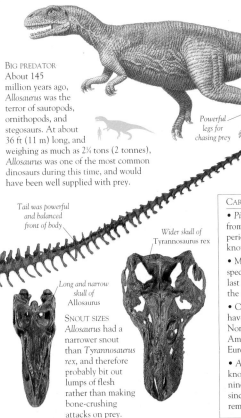

BIG PREDATOR
About 145 million years ago, *Allosaurus* was the terror of sauropods, ornithopods, and stegosaurs. At about 36 ft (11 m) long, and weighing as much as 2¼ tons (2 tonnes), *Allosaurus* was one of the most common dinosaurs during this time, and would have been well supplied with prey.

Thick tail

Powerful legs for chasing prey

Tail was powerful and balanced front of body

Wider skull of Tyrannosaurus rex

Long and narrow skull of Allosaurus

SNOUT SIZES
Allosaurus had a narrower snout than *Tyrannosaurus rex*, and therefore probably bit out lumps of flesh rather than making bone-crushing attacks on prey.

CARNOSAUR FACTS

• *Piatnitzkysaurus*, from the Jurassic period, is the oldest known carnosaur.

• Most carnosaur species existed in the last 10 million years of the Cretaceous period.

• Carnosaur remains have been found in North and South America, Asia, Africa, Europe, and Australia.

• *Allosaurus* has been known by more than nine different names since the first fossil remains were found.

CARNOTAURUS
HEAD

More carnosaurs

Fossilized remains of carnosaurs have been found worldwide. Many of the carnosaur skeletons that have been found are very incomplete. Consequently, they are difficult to study and understand, since pictures of whole dinosaurs have to be built up from small fragments of evidence. Scientists cannot even be sure that all of the dinosaurs they have grouped in the carnosaur group are, in fact, carnosaurs.

Tail held out to counterbalance front of body

GIGANOTOSAURUS

This South American discovery probably grew to a length of about 50 ft (15 m) – longer than the famous *Tyrannosaurus rex*. *Giganotosaurus* had a smaller brain and bigger hands than *Tyrannosaurus rex*, and was more closely related to *Allosaurus*. It may have weighed as much as 25 people.

Giganotosaurus may have preyed on large, plant-eating sauropods, such as Argentinosaurus.

Giganotosaurus could have weighed up to 9 tons (8 tonnes).

CARNOTAURUS
Found only in Argentina, *Carnotaurus*
was about 40 ft (12 m) long. Its short,
stubby head had the unusual feature of
two pointed horns above the eyes.
These horns may have been used
as weapons when fighting rivals.

*Rows of prominent,
ball-like scales ran along
the back and sides*

*Short, bony
horns*

*Sharp,
meat-eating
teeth*

FOSSIL TOOTH
This large carnosaur
tooth belonged to
Megalosaurus – the first
dinosaur to be named in
1824. Many fossils have
been wrongly identified
as *Megalosaurus* remains,
but very few real
Megalosaurus fossils
have been found.

*The cracks
occurred during
fossilization.*

*Very short,
weak arms cannot
have been of
much use*

*Powerful
rear legs*

ONE OF A KIND
The remains of only one
Eustreptospondylus have ever been
discovered. It is among many of the
carnosaurs whose fossils were
originally thought to belong to
Megalosaurus. Like other
carnosaurs, *Eustreptospondylus*
would have walked on its
three clawed toes.

Slender toes

Tyrannosaurids

Of all the carnosaurs, those in the tyrannosaurid family were the largest and probably the fiercest. The most famous member, *Tyrannosaurus rex*, was about 46 ft (14 m) long and 9 tons (8 tonnes) in weight. It is the largest land-based carnivore we know of. Tyrannosaurids not only caught and killed prey, they also scavenged dead creatures. They lived near the end of the Cretaceous period, and their remains have been found in North America and eastern Asia.

TYRANNOSAURUS REX TOOTH

Serrated edge

BIG TEETH
Tyrannosaurids had huge mouths, rimmed with huge, curved, serrated teeth. Some *Tyrannosaurus rex* teeth were 7 in (18 cm) long.

BIRD FOOT
The leg bones of *Tyrannosaurus rex* were thick and heavy to support its enormous weight. The metatarsal foot bones were locked into a single support, taking the weight above the three toes.

Knee

Tail raised for balance

Ankle

Metatarsals

Toe bones

Claws on end of toes

TYRANNOSAURUS REX
As the mightiest hunter, *Tyrannosaurus rex* would have had only another *Tyrannosaurus rex* to fear. But, like other animals, two *Tyrannosaurus rex* would have avoided confrontations, unless it was over females, territory, or food.

This hungry
Tyrannosaurus has
spotted another
Tyrannosaurus with
a meal.

TERRIBLE TEETH
Daspletosaurus had the massive jaw
typical of the tyrannosaurids, capable
of delivering a deadly blow in one
bite. Flesh and bones were sliced
and crushed by the
dagger-edged jaw.

A loud roar
warns intruder
to stay away

A weaker
Tyrannosaurus
might retreat
rather than
risk injury.

A fight between two
Tyrannosaurus
would be a ferocious
and bloody battle.

Clawed feet
pin the food to
the ground

Ornithomimosaurs

With their toothless beaks and slender feet, the ornithomimosaurs looked like giant, featherless birds. But their ostrichlike appearance also had the dinosaur features of clawed hands and a long tail. Ornithomimosaurs were long-necked and large – up to 16 ft (5 m) long. They were among the fastest dinosaurs, racing on slim and powerful rear legs. A wide mouth enabled them to swallow sizable prey, such as small mammals, as well as insects and fruits.

ORNITHOMIMOSAUR FACTS

• The name ornithomimosaur means "bird-mimic reptile."

• Ornithomimosaurs may have ran as fast as 43 mph (70 km/h).

• Predators: carnosaurs and dromaeosaurs

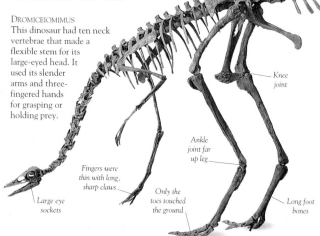

DROMICEIOMIMUS
This dinosaur had ten neck vertebrae that made a flexible stem for its large-eyed head. It used its slender arms and three-fingered hands for grasping or holding prey.

Knee joint

Ankle joint far up leg

Fingers were thin with long, sharp claws

Only the toes touched the ground

Long foot bones

Large eye sockets

LIKE AN OSTRICH
Struthiomimus had a similar running style to an ostrich. But unlike an ostrich, *Struthiomimus* had long, mobile arms which helped its clawed fingers grasp and hold prey. Its long tail was an important balancer at high speed.

Ostrich speed – up to 50mph (80 km/h)

Struthiomimus speed – less than 30 mph (50 km/h)

Three locked foot bones

FOOT AND LEG
As in all other ornithomimosaurs, the feet and legs of *Dromiceiomimus* were built to give fast acceleration. Only the toes touched the ground – the foot bones were locked into a single, birdlike extension of the leg.

Sharp claws

Long, flexible neck

Mobile wrist

GALLIMIMUS
The largest ornithomimosaur was *Gallimimus*. It had a long and narrow, snouted head with large eyes for good sight. Its weak jaws were covered by a sharp, horny beak.

Oviraptosaurs

The first oviraptosaur discovered had a crushed skull and was lying on a nest of fossilized dinosaur eggs. It was thought that it had been killed while trying to steal eggs from a *Protoceratops* nest, which is why it was given the name *Oviraptor*, meaning "egg stealer." We now know, however, that the eggs and nest belonged not to a *Protoceratops* but to the *Oviraptor* itself. Far from stealing the eggs, the *Oviraptor* probably died trying to protect them.

FOSSILIZED NEST OF
OVIRAPTOR EGGS

TRUE IDENTITY
Proof of the real nature of the "*Protoceratops*" eggs came when one of them was found to contain an *Oviraptor* embryo.

NEST DISCOVERY
Oviraptosaurs resembled large, flightless birds. In 1995, a fossilized *Oviraptor* was found sitting on its nest, as if brooding the eggs like a modern bird. The 18 eggs were laid in a circle in a hollow scooped out of a mound of sand.

Feathers

Toothless
beak

Sharp
claws

MODEL OF
OVIRAPTOR
ON NEST

Brightly
colored skin

OVIRAPTOSAUR FACTS

• Oviraptosaurs lived
near the end of the
Cretaceous period.

• Their large brain
cavity suggests that
they were intelligent.

• Most oviraptosaur
skeletons were found in
Mongolia, but recent
discoveries
have also been
made in England
and North America.

HEAD DECORATIONS
Many oviraptosaurs
had tall, bony head
crests. *Ingenia* lacked
a head crest, but it
might have had
brightly colored skin
instead.

Slender
skeleton

Muscle
on tail

SLIM AND AGILE
Oviraptosaurs were small
and lightly built, with hollow
bones. They had slim but
muscular back legs and
could run quite fast.
Their large hands had
curved fingers ending
in large, grasping claws.

Large
hands

OVIRAPTOR
MONGOLIENSIS
HEAD

Bony head
crest

*Cassowaries butt
their way through
vegetation when
escaping
from predators.*

HEAD CRESTS
Different oviraptosaurs
had differently shaped
crests. A modern bird, the
cassowary, has a crest to
butt its way through
forest undergrowth.
Perhaps oviraptosaurs used their
crest for a similar purpose.

CASSOWARY
HEAD

Troodontids

Near the end of the Cretaceous period, a very rare group of dinosaurs appeared. Scientists have called them troodontids. Although their body design was similar to the ornithomimosaurs, they were a distinct group of theropods. Troodontids had large brains for their body size. This, coupled with well-developed senses, has given them the reputation as the most intelligent of the dinosaurs.

Slender head perched on long neck

The troodontids are now thought to have been feathered, rather than scaly-skinned.

Serrated edge

TROODON
The best-known troodontid is *Troodon*. It had a light and delicate skeleton with slim rear limbs. Troodontid fossils are rare, partly because their thin bones were not easily preserved.

SHARP EDGE
Troodon had a long, narrow mouth lined with curved and serrated bladelike teeth.

Long, slender leg bones

FAST RUNNER
Troodon could run very fast on its long back legs. It probably chased small prey such as insects, small mammals, lizards, and baby dinosaurs.

Elongated foot bones lengthened legs

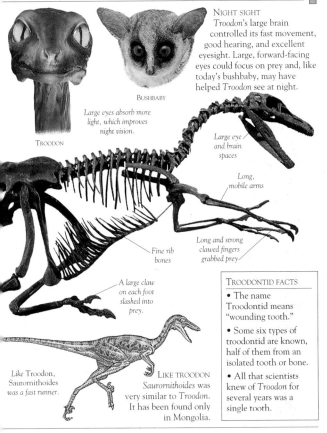

NIGHT SIGHT

Troodon's large brain controlled its fast movement, good hearing, and excellent eyesight. Large, forward-facing eyes could focus on prey and, like today's bushbaby, may have helped *Troodon* see at night.

BUSHBABY

Large eyes absorb more light, which improves night vision.

TROODON

Large eye and brain spaces

Long, mobile arms

Long and strong clawed fingers grabbed prey

Fine rib bones

A large claw on each foot slashed into prey.

TROODONTID FACTS

• The name Troodontid means "wounding tooth."

• Some six types of troodontid are known, half of them from an isolated tooth or bone.

• All that scientists knew of *Troodon* for several years was a single tooth.

Like Troodon, Saurornithoides was a fast runner.

LIKE TROODON *Saurornithoides* was very similar to *Troodon*. It has been found only in Mongolia.

Dromaeosaurids

These razor-toothed carnivores were very agile and had large brains and huge eyes with stereoscopic vision. They were among the most terrifying of all dinosaurs. A large sickle-shaped talon on their inner toes could rotate through 180°, slicing into their prey's tough hide.

Sharp teeth

Eye socket

Rigid tail

DROMAEOSAURUS SKULL
The skull of *Dromaeosaurus* shows that it had sharp teeth, large, forward-pointing eyes for judging distance, and a large brain that suggests that it was intelligent.

Some of the Deinonychus pack might die during an attack.

DROMAEOSAURID FACTS

• The name dromaeosaurid means "swift-running reptile."

• They are thought to be among the most intelligent and agile of the dinosaurs.

• The largest were up to 6½ ft (2 m) tall.

• They lived in the Cretaceous period.

PACK HUNTING
Deinonychus hunted in packs, bringing down prey with their sharp-clawed hands and slashing talons. A combined attack meant that they could kill prey much larger than themselves, such as the herbivore *Tenontosaurus*.

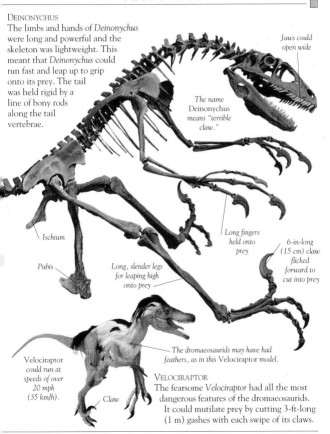

DEINONYCHUS

The limbs and hands of *Deinonychus* were long and powerful and the skeleton was lightweight. This meant that *Deinonychus* could run fast and leap up to grip onto its prey. The tail was held rigid by a line of bony rods along the tail vertebrae.

Jaws could open wide

The name Deinonychus means "terrible claw."

Ischium

Pubis

Long fingers held onto prey

6-in-long (15 cm) claw flicked forward to cut into prey

Long, slender legs for leaping high onto prey

The dromaeosaurids may have had feathers, as in this Velociraptor model.

Velociraptor could run at speeds of over 20 mph (35 km/h).

Claw

VELOCIRAPTOR

The fearsome *Velociraptor* had all the most dangerous features of the dromaeosaurids. It could mutilate prey by cutting 3-ft-long (1 m) gashes with each swipe of its claws.

Spinosaurids

COMPSOGNATHUS
SKULL

This group of large, fish-eating theropods existed throughout the Cretaceous period. *Spinosaurus*, was found in 1915, but the specimen was destroyed during World War II. With the discovery of new spinosaurids since the 1980s, such as *Suchomimus* and *Baryonyx*, scientists are gaining a clearer idea of what they were really like.

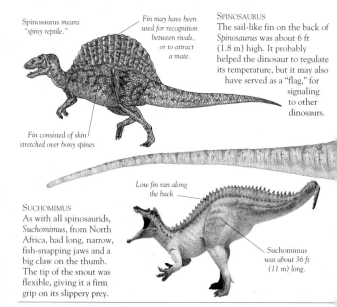

Spinosaurus *means
"spiny reptile."*

Fin may have been
used for recognition
between rivals,
or to attract
a mate.

Fin consisted of skin
stretched over bony spines

SPINOSAURUS
The sail-like fin on the back of *Spinosaurus* was about 6 ft (1.8 m) high. It probably helped the dinosaur to regulate its temperature, but it may also have served as a "flag," for signaling to other dinosaurs.

Low fin ran along
the back

SUCHOMIMUS
As with all spinosaurids, *Suchomimus*, from North Africa, had long, narrow, fish-snapping jaws and a big claw on the thumb. The tip of the snout was flexible, giving it a firm grip on its slippery prey.

Suchomimus
was about 36 ft
(11 m) long.

UNIQUE SKELETON
We know about *Baryonyx* from a single skeleton, which includes a 6-in- (30-cm-) long thumb claw. Its crocodile-like snout, which had a crest on top, had 128 finely serrated teeth. The main diet of *Baryonyx* may have been fish, which it could snatch from the river using its long claws.

Lower jaw

The Baryonyx skeleton that was found was only 70 percent complete.

Clawed foot

BARYONYX
Baryonyx would have been about 10.5 m (34 ft) long and nearly 3 m (10 ft) tall. It held its head low, and its neck was straight, not curved like many other theropods.

Crocodile-like snout

Neck held straight

DEATH POSE
This reconstruction of *Baryonyx* shows how it must have looked shortly after dying.

Powerful legs

DINOSAURS AND BIRDS

SURPRISING THOUGH IT might seem, scientists now recognize birds as the closest living relatives of dinosaurs. The most primitive bird is *Archaeopteryx*. In 1861, an *Archaeopteryx* skeleton together with fossil impressions of its feathers were found in a quarry in Germany. *Archaeopteryx* lived about 140 million years ago, alongside the dinosaurs that it resembled in many ways.

Birdlike feathers, tail, and wings

Dinosaur-like skull, hips, and feet

Wings were too small for flight

CAUDIPTERYX
Since the late 1990s, all sorts of half-bird/half-dinosaur fossils have come to light from Jurassic and Cretaceous lake deposits in China. *Caudipteryx* is one of these discoveries.

Lightweight skull

Short body

COMPSOGNATHUS SKELETON

Long tail

Short body

Long tail

Long, slender leg bone

Long fingers

Elongated foot bone

SIMILARITIES
Small theropod dinosaurs, such as *Compsognathus*, had many features in common with *Archaeopteryx*. These included a lightweight skull, a short body, long, thin limbs, and in some theropods, a wishbone. This helps confirm their close relationship.

ARCHAEOPTERYX SKELETON

ARCHAEOPTERYX FOSSIL
This fossil skeleton of *Archaeopteryx* was found in 1877 in Germany. Fossil impressions left by the feathers can be seen clearly. *Archaeopteryx* was a carnivore. It ate small animals and insects.

FLIGHTS
Archaeopteryx may have spent a lot of time in trees, from which it would have launched itself into flight.

Clawed hands – a feature modern birds do not have

Delicate impressions of wing feathers

Skull

Tail feather impressions

Clawed foot

Long, dinosaur-like tail

The feathers of Archaeopteryx were similar to those of modern pigeons.

ARCHAEOPTERYX FACTS
• The name *Archaeopteryx* means "ancient wing."

• *Archaeopteryx* was about 2 ft (60 cm) long.

• Lived toward the end of the Jurassic period.

• *Archaeopteryx* skeletons have been found only in Germany.

SAUROPODOMORPHS

TWO GROUPS, the prosauropods and
the sauropods, are included in the
sauropodomorphs. Unlike the theropods,
most sauropodomorphs were
quadrupedal (walked on four legs) and
were herbivores. They had long necks
and tails, and ranged in size from 6½ ft
(2 m) to 130 ft (40 m) in length.

APATOSAURUS
THUMB CLAW

THUMB CLAW
Many sauropodomorphs
had big, curved thumb
claws. They probably
used these dangerous
weapons for
defense.

*Long,
flexible
neck*

*Large front
feet could
hold plants
when feeding*

*Prosauropods such
as Plateosaurus
were the first large
land animals.*

Plateosaurus
may have often
walked on only
two legs.

PLATEOSAURUS
Several complete skeletons of the
prosauropod *Plateosaurus* have been
found. It is one of the earliest and
largest saurischian dinosaurs of the
Triassic period. Although
quadrupedal, it could probably
stand on its hind legs to reach up
to feed on the higher branches.

*Small
skull*

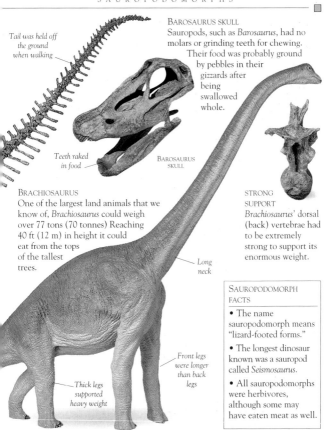

Tail was held off the ground when walking

BAROSAURUS SKULL
Sauropods, such as *Barosaurus*, had no molars or grinding teeth for chewing. Their food was probably ground by pebbles in their gizzards after being swallowed whole.

Teeth raked in food

BAROSAURUS SKULL

BRACHIOSAURUS
One of the largest land animals that we know of, *Brachiosaurus* could weigh over 77 tons (70 tonnes) Reaching 40 ft (12 m) in height it could eat from the tops of the tallest trees.

STRONG SUPPORT
Brachiosaurus' dorsal (back) vertebrae had to be extremely strong to support its enormous weight.

Long neck

Front legs were longer than back legs

Thick legs supported heavy weight

SAUROPODOMORPH FACTS

• The name sauropodomorph means "lizard-footed forms."

• The longest dinosaur known was a sauropod called *Seismosaurus.*

• All sauropodomorphs were herbivores, although some may have eaten meat as well.

Prosauropods

The prosauropods are thought to be close ancestors of the sauropods. Both groups have long necks and small heads, but the prosauropods were generally smaller in size. Most prosauropods were herbivores, although some may have been omnivores (eating both meat and plants).

MASSOSPONDYLUS THUMB CLAW

THUMB CLAW
Massospondylus may have been an omnivore since it had large, serrated front teeth. It also had sharp thumb claws, which it may have used to attack prey, as well as for defense.

Teeth

Eye socket

SMALL SKULL
Riojasaurus, at 33 ft (10 m) in length, was the largest prosauropod. As with other prosauropods, its skull was tiny compared to its massive body, and its jaws were lined with leaf-shaped teeth for shredding plant food.

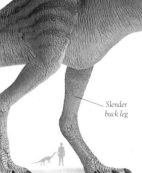

ANCHISAURUS
This prosauropod was designed to walk on all fours, but it may have occasionally run on two feet. *Anchisaurus* had large, sickle-shaped thumb claws which would have been dangerous weapons against attackers.

Slender back leg

PROSAUROPOD FACTS

• The name prosauropod means "before sauropods."

• All prosauropods had small heads, long necks, and long tails.

• *Plateosaurus* was the first large dinosaur.

• Their remains have been found worldwide, except Antarctica.

VIEW FROM ABOVE
This view from above of *Anchisaurus* shows that its body was long and slender. It would have held its tail off the ground when walking.

Slim and flexible neck

REACHING HIGH
Plateosaurus was one of the earliest and largest saurischian dinosaurs. It grew to about 26 ft (8 m) in length, and could stand on its hind legs to reach tall trees when feeding.

Lower arm

Large thumb claw

Thumb claw

PULLING CLAW
The toes on the hands of *Plateosaurus* varied greatly in length. The thumb, the largest, ended with a huge, sharp claw.

Sauropods

The largest-ever land animals were included in the sauropod group. Sauropods were quadrupedal, plant-eating saurischian dinosaurs. They all had huge bodies with long necks and elephant-like legs. They also had long tails which they used as whiplike weapons against enemies.

TAIL REINFORCEMENT
Tail bones like the one above were on the underside of *Diplodocus'* tail. They reinforced and protected the tail when it was pressed against the ground.

Back of jaws was toothless

Peglike teeth

FRONT TEETH
Diplodocus had a long skull with peglike teeth at the front of the jaws. The teeth would have raked in plants such as cycads, ginkgoes, and conifers. *Diplodocus* had no back teeth, so the food was probably ground in the stomach by gastroliths (stomach stones).

APATOSAURUS
Once called *Brontosaurus*, this dinosaur was one of the largest sauropods, at 73 ft (23 m) long and weighing 30 tons (27 tonnes). It had a horselike head with a fist-sized brain, and powerful legs with padded feet.

Tail would have been held off the ground

Tail contained 82 bones

TAIL WEAPON
Barosaurus resembled *Diplodocus*, but had a slightly longer neck and a shorter tail. The narrow tail may have been a defense weapon.

Tail may have been used like a whip against enemies

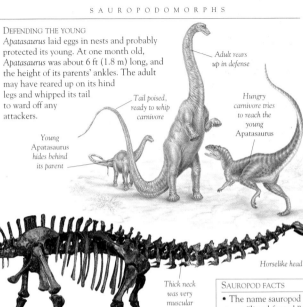

DEFENDING THE YOUNG
Apatasaurus laid eggs in nests and probably
protected its young. At one month old,
Apatasaurus was about 6 ft (1.8 m) long, and
the height of its parents' ankles. The adult
may have reared up on its hind
legs and whipped its tail
to ward off any
attackers.

*Adult rears
up in defense*

*Tail poised,
ready to whip
carnivore*

*Hungry
carnivore tries
to reach the
young
Apatasaurus*

*Young
Apatasaurus
hides behind
its parent*

Horselike head

*Thick neck
was very
muscular*

NECK BONE
Some of *Barosaurus*' neck
bones were over 3 ft (1 m)
in length. The bones were
hollowed out to reduce the weight
of the 30-ft-long (9 m) neck.

SAUROPOD FACTS
• The name sauropod
means "lizard footed."

• All sauropods were
herbivores.

• Sauropods may have
moved at up to 2½ mph
(4 km/h).

• Many types of
sauropod traveled in
herds.

• Some may have lived
for up to 100 years.

More sauropods

Scientists used to think that the ankylosaurs were the only armored dinosaurs. But the discovery of *Saltasaurus* proved that some sauropods had armor, too. It was also thought that sauropods may have lived in water, but we now know that the high water pressure at depth would not have allowed them to breathe.

SHORT SKULL
The short and high skull of *Camarasaurus* has a very large orbit (eye socket) and naris (nostril socket). There are approximately 48 spoonlike teeth.

SALTASAURUS
At 39 ft (12 m) long, *Saltasaurus* was quite small for a sauropod. Its armor consisted of large, bony plates surrounded by smaller bony scutes. The armor possibly covered *Saltasaurus'* back and sides. The group of armored sauropods is called the titanosaurids.

Shunosaurus grew to about 33 ft (10 m) in length.

Enemies may have been battered by the tail club.

SHUNOSAURUS
This sauropod from China had a spiked club on the end of its tail, which it presumably used for self-defense.

MAMENCHISAURUS
Another Chinese sauropod, *Mamenchisaurus*, had the longest neck known in any animal. Containing 19 neck vertebrae, it measured about 46 ft (14 m) long, making up more than half the animal's entire length.

CETIOSAURUS
An early sauropod, *Cetiosaurus* had massive, heavy, and solid. Later sauropods had bones that were light and hollow.

Cetiosaurus was the first sauropod to be discovered.

Cetiosaurus may have weighed as much as five elephants.

Thick legs to support enormous weight

SCUTES
Only randomly scattered scutes of *Saltasaurus* have been found, so we have to guess at their position on its body.

Bony lumps

SKIN IMPRESSION
Parts of the body of *Saltasaurus* were protected by a covering of tightly packed, pea-sized, bony lumps.

ORNITHISCHIAN DINOSAURS

ABOUT ORNITHISCHIANS

THERE WERE FIVE main groups of ornithischians. They were all herbivores with hoofed feet and hipbones arranged like modern birds. They also had beaked mouths, apart from those in the pachycephalosaur group. Ornithischians were either bipedal or quadrupedal. Bipedal ornithischians had stiffened tails to counterbalance their bodies while feeding or running.

CERATOPSIANS

ANKYLOSAURS

ORNITHOPODS

PACHYCEPHALOSAURS

STEGOSAURS

FIVE GROUPS
The five groups of ornithischians were: ceratopsians, with their neck frills; ankylosaurs, with their body armor; pachycephalosaurs, with their domed heads; stegosaurs, with their back plates, and the birdlike ornithopods.

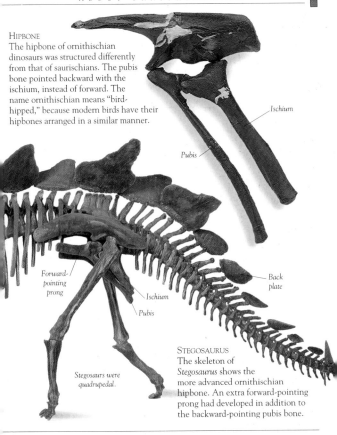

HIPBONE

The hipbone of ornithischian dinosaurs was structured differently from that of saurischians. The pubis bone pointed backward with the ischium, instead of forward. The name ornithischian means "bird-hipped," because modern birds have their hipbones arranged in a similar manner.

Ischium

Pubis

Forward-pointing prong

Back plate

Ischium

Pubis

STEGOSAURUS

The skeleton of *Stegosaurus* shows the more advanced ornithischian hipbone. An extra forward-pointing prong had developed in addition to the backward-pointing pubis bone.

Stegosaurs were quadrupedal.

STEGOSAURS

THE MOST NOTICEABLE features of the stegosaurs were the large plates, or spines, along an arched back. These plates may have regulated body temperature, and they may have also given protection, or even attracted a mate. Stegosaurs had small heads, and tiny brains no larger than a golf ball. The head was carried close to the ground for eating short, leafy plants and fruits.

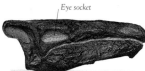

Eye socket

STEGOSAURUS SKULL
The skull of *Stegosaurus* was long and narrow. It had a toothless beak and small cheek teeth for chewing vegetation.

TAIL END
Stegosaurus is the most commonly known of all stegosaurs. It had long, horny spines on the end of its tail. With a quick swing of the tail, these spines could inflict a crippling stab to a predator, such as *Allosaurus*.

Spines had a sharp end.

PLATES AND SPINES
From above you can see the staggered plates along the top of *Stegosaurus*' body. This view also shows the tail spines pointing backward and outward – protection against attack from behind for when *Stegosaurus* was escaping.

Backward-pointing spines

Staggered plates

STEGOSAUR FACTS

• The name stegosaur means "plated reptile."

• Stegosaurs ranged in size from 15 ft (4.5 m) to 29½ ft (9 m).

• The stegosaur group survived for over 50 million years.

• They ate only certain plants, probably seed ferns and cycads.

• All stegosaurs had tail spines for defense.

STEGOSAURUS

The plates on *Stegosaurus*' back were tallest in the region of the hips, reaching about 2½ ft (75 cm) in height. From a distance, or in silhouette, the plates may have made *Stegosaurus* look much bigger than it really was, thus acting as a deterrent to predators.

Plates were tallest above hips

FOSSIL PLATE
This fossil plate was one of the small plates at the front of *Stegosaurus*. The plates were thin and made of bone, and contained a network of blood vessels.

Small head

More stegosaurs

The front legs of stegosaurs were shorter than the rear legs. Stegosaurs may have reared up on their hind legs, balancing with their tail on the ground. The supple tail and powerful rear legs could have formed a tripod allowing stegosaurs to reach higher vegetation. The plates and spines may have been used for different purposes in different stegosaurs.

Cast of "second brain"

Cast of brain in skull

TUOJIANGOSAURUS
Some scientists believe this reconstructed skeleton of *Tuojiangosaurus* to
be wrong. They think the front limbs
should be straighter, and not bent like
a lizard's.

TWO BRAINS
It was once believed that stegosaurs had a
second brain which filled a large cavity in
the hips. But this is now known to have
been a nerve center, which controlled
the hind limbs and the tail.

Large spines
for wounding
enemies

Tail was
held off the
ground

KENTROSAURUS
Six pairs of bony plates
ran along the neck and
shoulders of *Kentrosaurus*. Behind
these plates were three pairs of flat
spines and five pairs of long, sharp spines.

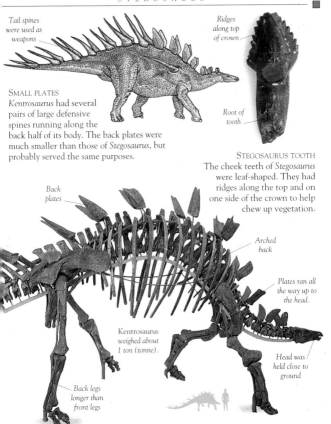

Tail spines were used as weapons

Ridges along top of crown

SMALL PLATES
Kentrosaurus had several pairs of large defensive spines running along the back half of its body. The back plates were much smaller than those of *Stegosaurus*, but probably served the same purposes.

Root of tooth

STEGOSAURUS TOOTH
The cheek teeth of *Stegosaurus* were leaf-shaped. They had ridges along the top and on one side of the crown to help chew up vegetation.

Back plates

Arched back

Plates ran all the way up to the head.

Kentrosaurus weighed about 1 ton (tonne).

Head was held close to ground

Back legs longer than front legs

ANKYLOSAURS

PROTECTED BY SPIKES and bony plates, the stocky ankylosaurs were the armored tanks of the dinosaur world. There were two main groups of ankylosaurs – the ankylosaurids and the nodosaurids.

SKULL
The triangular skull of *Ankylosaurus* was covered with bony plates. It ended at a horny beak, which it used to crop vegetation.

Ankylosaurids

Many ankylosaurids had spines on their sides as well as bony body scutes (plates). Their most notable feature was a heavy tail club, which they used as a formidable weapon.

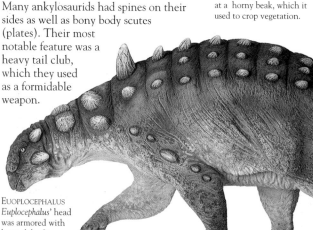

EUOPLOCEPHALUS
Euoplocephalus' head was armored with bony slabs. Its eyelids were bony too, protecting the vulnerable eyes. The stout body and tail club were typical of ankylosaurids.

ANKYLOSAUR FACTS

• The name ankylosaur means "armored reptile."

• They ranged in length from 6 ft (1.8 m) to 29½ ft (9 m).

• They have been found on all continents, including Antarctica.

• All were covered in bony scutes on their upper side, but were unarmored on their lower side.

TAIL CLUB
The bony plates were good protection, but the tail club was an extremely effective weapon. A fearsome tyrannosaurid could be crippled with a well-directed blow to the ankle or shin.

Tyrannosaurus receives a crippling blow

Ankylosaur lashes out at the knee

TAIL CLUB
The tail club was formed by bony plates that were fused together. Powerful tail muscles were used to swing the club. These muscles were anchored by tail vertebrae stiffened by bony tendons.

FOSSILIZED ANKYLOSAURID TAIL CLUB

Euoplocephalus was about 23 ft (7 m) long.

Stiffened, muscular tail

Heavy tail club

Nodosaurids

Armored with bony plates and dangerous spikes, but lacking the clubbed tail of the ankylosaurids, the nodosaurids were the most primitive of the ankylosaurs. They ranged in size from 5 ft (1.6 m) to 25 ft (7.6 m) in length. Nodosaurid fossils have been found in rocks worldwide.

Gap between jaws for cheek pouch

Plates on top of skull

SHEEPLIKE SKULL
The pear-shaped skull of *Edmontonia* resembles that of a sheep. It had cheek pouches in which to store food. The top of the skull was reinforced with bony plates for protection.

Crown of tooth with ridged edge

GROUND GRAZER
Edmontonia had small, weak teeth on the sides of its jaws. They were leaf-shaped and flattened – ideal for chopping up leafy vegetation.

Root of tooth

EDMONTONIA
One of the largest of the nodosaurids, *Edmontonia* probably grew to about 23 ft (7 m) in length. Long spikes lined the sides and shoulders, and tough neck plates protected it from tyrannosaurid fangs.

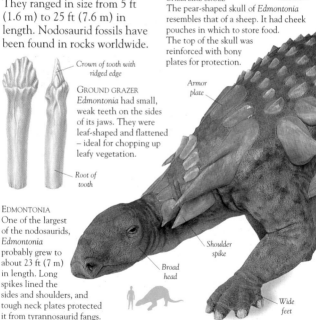

Armor plate

Shoulder spike

Broad head

Wide feet

SAUROPELTA
An armor of spikes, bony cones, and small studs
stretched along the back and tail of *Sauropelta*. Its
underside was unprotected, so it may
have crouched close to the
ground when
under attack.

Bony
cones

Bony
studs

Shoulder
spikes

Soft,
vulnerable
underside

Short,
stubby
legs

ROWS OF PLATES
Sauropelta's cone-shaped
plates lay in rows, similar to
the bands of armor on a
modern giant armadillo.

Stout,
strong
legs

Armored
tail

Spines on
back

Spines on
tail

POLACANTHUS
Two rows of spines jutted out
of *Polacanthus'* back. There
were also two rows of triangular
bony scutes along its tail.

105

ORNITHOPODS

ALL THE ORNITHOPOD dinosaurs were herbivores with horned beaks. Their jaws and leaf-shaped cheek teeth were ideal for chewing vegetation. They were bipedal, although some of them may have foraged for food on all fours. Their feet had three or four toes with hooflike claws, and their hands had four or five fingers.

Cheek teeth

Tusklike teeth

TOOTHY SKULL
Heterodontosaurus had three different kinds of teeth. These were the front upper teeth, which bit against the toothless lower beak; the scissorlike cheek teeth; and a pair of upper and lower tusklike teeth.

GROUP LIVING
Hypsilophodon may have moved in herds for protection against predatory theropods. Moving as a large group, they would have been able to warn each other of any danger, giving them a better chance of survival.

Group members looked from side to side for any danger.

Slim, long legs for speed

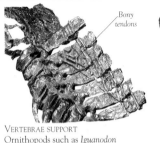

Bony tendons

VERTEBRAE SUPPORT
Ornithopods such as *Iguanodon* had a crisscross of bony tendons strengthening the vertebrae above the hip and in the back. These bony tendons also stiffened the tail. This helped *Iguanodon* balance as it walked on its two back legs.

ORNITHOPOD FACTS
• The name ornithopod means "bird foot."
• They ranged in length from 6½ ft (2 m) to 49 ft (15 m).
• Some ornithopods had up to 1,000 cheek teeth.
• They could run at speeds of at least 15 mph (9 km/h).

THREE-TOED FEET
The powerful three-toed feet of *Corythosaurus* were built to carry its heavy weight. *Corythosaurus* weighed approximately 4½ tons (4 tonnes) and was about 24 ft (7.5 m) long. It belonged to a group of ornithopods called hadrosaurs.

Toes ended in flattened hooves

Hypsilophodon was about 7½ ft (2.3 m) long.

Iguanodonts

These dinosaurs were bipedal herbivores with long toes that ended in hooflike claws. Their arms were thick and strong, and they may have often walked on all fours, perhaps when foraging for food. Iguanodonts had a single row of tall, ridged teeth, with which they chewed their food before swallowing it. The best-known iguanodonts are *Iguanodon* and *Ouranosaurus*.

Ridges on edge of tooth

Worn-down tooth

WEAR AND TEAR
The *Iguanodon* teeth above are at different stages of wear. The one on the right has been worn down by *Iguanodon*'s diet of tough plants, while the one on the left looks like it has hardly been used.

IGUANODON STABBING A THEROPOD IN THE NECK

STABBING WEAPON
Iguanodon had large, bony thumb spikes. These may have been used as weapons against enemies, such as theropods. *Iguanodon* may have used its thumb spike to stab an attacker through the throat, belly, or eyes.

IGUANODON
The head of *Iguanodon* had a toothless beak for nipping vegetation. Its arms were much shorter than its hind legs, which ended in strong, three-toed feet to support its heavy weight. Its thick tail was very stiff, and was held out almost horizontally.

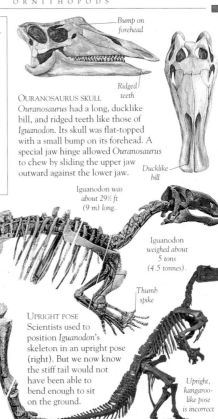

• The name iguanodont means "iguana tooth."

• They ranged in length from 13 ft (4 m) to 29½ ft (9 m).

• They lived from late Jurassic through to late Cretaceous periods.

• An *Iguanodon* shin bone found in 1809 was not identified as belonging to *Iguanodon* until the late 1970s.

Bump on forehead

Ridged teeth

OURANOSAURUS SKULL
Ouranosaurus had a long, ducklike bill, and ridged teeth like those of *Iguanodon*. Its skull was flat-topped with a small bump on its forehead. A special jaw hinge allowed *Ouranosaurus* to chew by sliding the upper jaw outward against the lower jaw.

Ducklike bill

Iguanodon was about 29½ ft (9 m) long.

Iguanodon weighed about 5 tons (4.5 tonnes).

Thumb spike

UPRIGHT POSE
Scientists used to position *Iguanodon*'s skeleton in an upright pose (right). But we now know the stiff tail would not have been able to bend enough to sit on the ground.

Knee

Ankle

Upright, kangaroo-like pose is incorrect

Hadrosaurs

These herbivores are also known as "duckbills," because of their toothless, ducklike bills. Hundreds of self-sharpening teeth arranged in rows lined the sides of the jaws. Hadrosaurs were bipedal. They held their bodies horizontally with their stiffened tails extended for balance. There are two main groups of hadrosaurs: hadrosaurines, with flat-topped skulls, and lambeosaurines, with hollow head crests.

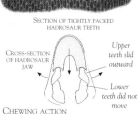

SECTION OF TIGHTLY PACKED HADROSAUR TEETH

CROSS-SECTION OF HADROSAUR JAW

Upper teeth slid outward

Lower teeth did not move

CHEWING ACTION
Hadrosaurs chewed food by grating the upper jaw teeth against the lower jaw teeth. The upper jaw was hinged so that when the jaws closed, the upper jaw would slide outward against the lower jaw.

Bony rods along spine

Deep tail

This Gryposaurus skeleton was found in Alberta, Canada.

HADROSAUR FACTS
• The name hadrosaur means "bulky lizard."

• They ranged in length from 10 ft (3 m) to 49 ft (15 m).

• They are known as the duck-billed dinosaurs because of their long, flat snouts.

GRYPOSAURUS
Like many hadrosaurs, *Gryposaurus* had a trellis of bony rods that stiffened the spine and tail. Above the duck-like bill, the nasal bones formed a distinctive bump. In life, this was probably covered in skin and, flushed with blood, could have been used as a color signal.

CORYTHOSAURUS

Although *Corythosaurus* was bipedal, the hoof-shaped claws and padded toes on its hands indicate that it used them a lot for walking. Its diet included the toughest of plants, such as ferns and pine needles, but *Corythosaurus* could easily mash these using its rows of tightly packed teeth.

Hands could hold onto branches

Corythosaurus walked on all fours when feeding on ground-level plants.

Stiff tail was held out horizontally

Hadrosaurines

This group of hadrosaurs had little or no head crest, although some had a bump above the nose which they used for making noises. Some hadrosaurines had bills that curled upward, forming a spoon shape. They lived in North America, Europe, and Asia during the late Cretaceous period.

HADROSAUR FAMILY
Maiasaura bred in huge colonies, using the same nesting sites every year. The name *Maiasaura* means "good mother lizard"; *Maiasaura* cared for their young until they could fend for themselves.

Male *Maiasaura* feeding young

Eggs were laid in a mound made of earth and plant material

Female watches eggs

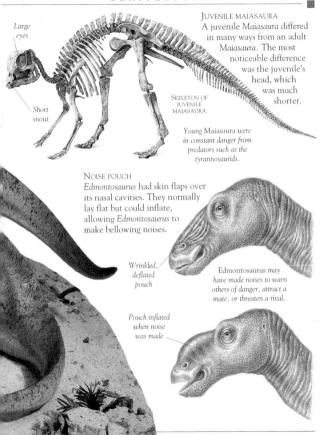

Large
eyes

Short
snout

JUVENILE MAIASAURA

A juvenile *Maiasaura* differed in many ways from an adult *Maiasaura*. The most noticeable difference was the juvenile's head, which was much shorter.

SKELETON OF
JUVENILE
MAIASAURA

*Young Maiasaura were
in constant danger from
predators such as the
tyrannosaurids.*

NOISE POUCH

Edmontosaurus had skin flaps over its nasal cavities. They normally lay flat but could inflate, allowing *Edmontosaurus* to make bellowing noises.

Wrinkled,
deflated
pouch

*Edmontosaurus may
have made noises to warn
others of danger, attract a
mate, or threaten a rival.*

Pouch inflated
when noise
was made

Lambeosaurines

Large bony head crests were a distinctive feature of these hadrosaurs. Powerful limbs supported a heavy body, and the downward-curving lower jaw had a broad, blunt beak. They lived around the same time as the hadrosaurines, and their remains have been found in North America and Asia.

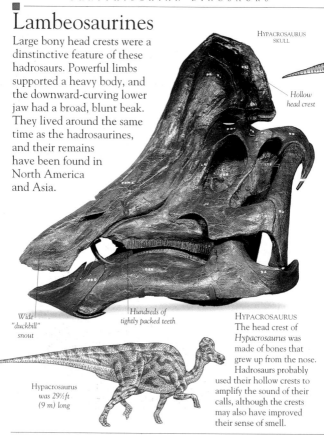

HYPACROSAURUS SKULL

Hollow head crest

Wide "duckbill" snout

Hundreds of tightly packed teeth

Hypacrosaurus was 29½ ft (9 m) long

HYPACROSAURUS
The head crest of *Hypacrosaurus* was made of bones that grew up from the nose. Hadrosaurs probably used their hollow crests to amplify the sound of their calls, although the crests may also have improved their sense of smell.

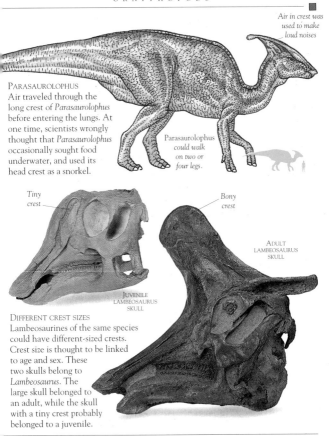

Air in crest was used to make loud noises

PARASAUROLOPHUS
Air traveled through the long crest of *Parasaurolophus* before entering the lungs. At one time, scientists wrongly thought that *Parasaurolophus* occasionally sought food underwater, and used its head crest as a snorkel.

Parasaurolophus could walk on two or four legs.

Tiny crest

Bony crest

ADULT LAMBEOSAURUS SKULL

JUVENILE LAMBEOSAURUS SKULL

DIFFERENT CREST SIZES
Lambeosaurines of the same species could have different-sized crests. Crest size is thought to be linked to age and sex. These two skulls belong to *Lambeosaurus*. The large skull belonged to an adult, while the skull with a tiny crest probably belonged to a juvenile.

PACHYCEPHALOSAURS

THE THICK, DOMED skulls of pachycephalosaurs earned them the name "bone-headed dinosaurs." Rival males used to bash their heads together, their brains protected by the thick bone. Pachycephalosaurs probably had a good sense of smell, which would have allowed them to detect nearby predators and escape before the predators got too close.

HORN CLUSTER
Stygimoloch had a cluster of horns behind its dome. But the horns were probably just for show, rather than of practical use.

LOTS OF BUMPS
Prenocephale's head had a well-developed solid dome and small bumps on the back of the skull.

PACHYCEPHALOSAUR FACTS

• The name pachycephalosaur means "thick-headed lizard."

• They ranged in length from 3 ft (90 cm) to 15 ft (4.6 m).

• Diet included fruits, leaves, and insects.

STEGOCERAS
Goat-sized *Stegoceras* was about 8 ft (2.4 m) long. Several *Stegoceras* skulls have been found with domes of various thicknesses. The domes of juveniles were not as thick or high as those of adults, especially adult males.

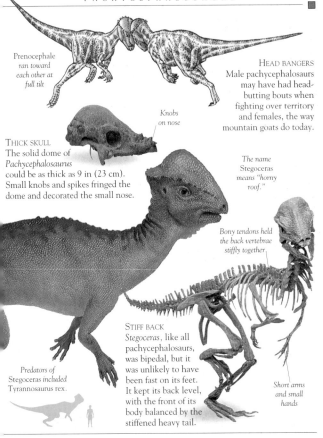

Prenocephale
ran toward
each other at
full tilt

HEAD BANGERS
Male pachycephalosaurs
may have had head-
butting bouts when
fighting over territory
and females, the way
mountain goats do today.

Knobs
on nose

THICK SKULL
The solid dome of
Pachycephalosaurus
could be as thick as 9 in (23 cm).
Small knobs and spikes fringed the
dome and decorated the small nose.

The name
Stegoceras
means "horny
roof."

Bony tendons held
the back vertebrae
stiffly together

STIFF BACK
Stegoceras, like all
pachycephalosaurs,
was bipedal, but it
was unlikely to have
been fast on its feet.
It kept its back level,
with the front of its
body balanced by the
stiffened heavy tail.

Predators of
Stegoceras included
Tyrannosaurus rex.

Short arms
and small
hands

CERATOPSIANS

HORNS, BONY FRILLS, and a
parrotlike beak were the trade-
marks of the ceratopsians. They
were all quadrupedal herbivores,
and many ceratopsians lived in great
herds. Most ceratopsians can be divided
into two groups. One group had short neck frills, the
other had long neck frills. The ceratopsians were
among the last dinosaurs to
become extinct.

PSITTACOSAURUS
SKULL

Psittacosaurus
may have moved
on all fours
when foraging.

PSITTACOSAURUS
This dinosaur was a 6½-ft-long
(2 m) bipedal ancestor of
the ceratopsians. It had
a parrotlike beak
and a very
small neck frill,
but lacked the horns
of ceratopsians.

PROTOCERATOPS

This dinosaur was the first true ceratopsian, with a turtlelike beak and a small frill. *Protoceratops* roamed the plains of central Asia in herds.

Bony frill stuck out over the neck

Decorative frill

Horns scared off attackers

Nose horn was short and blunt

Rostral bone is inside the beak

TRICERATOPS

Among the ceratopsians, *Triceratops* was one of the last and the largest. Herds of *Triceratops* roamed through forests, chopping vegetation with their beaks. The beak was supported by a rostral bone, which was common to all ceratopsians.

Short-frilled ceratopsians

The group of ceratopsians with short frills also had long nose horns and short brow horns. *Styracosaurus* had the most dramatic frill, with long horns growing out from its edge. The discovery of five young near an adult *Brachyceratops* indicates that these ceratopsians looked after their young. It is likely that when a herd was in danger from predators, the males protected the young and the females.

STYRACOSAURUS SKULL

Long nose horn

STYRACOSAURUS
Six long spikes edged the frill of *Styracosaurus*. It had a lethal horn on its nose that was 2 ft (60 cm) long and 6 in (15 cm) thick. The horns above the eyes, however, were only stumps. It was possibly a good runner, capable of speeds of up to 20 mph (32 km/h).

Horns on edge of frill

Nose horn

FOSSIL BEAK
Ceratopsian dinosaurs had beaks that were ideal for slicing through twigs and tough plants. Each beak had a horny covering that was attached to the grooves and pits on the surface.

Horny covering was attached to grooves on surface

Bony hook

Stumps along edge of frill

CENTROSAURUS
The horn on the nose of *Centrosaurus* curved forward rather than backward like most other ceratopsians. The short frill had small stumps along the edge, as well as a pair of long central hooks which projected forward.

A rhinocerous has two horns on its nose.

SIMILAR BODIES
Rhinoceroses resemble ceratopsians with their stocky bodies and facial horns. A charging rhinoceros reaches speeds of up to 28 mph (45 km/h), and it is thought that ceratopsians such as *Centrosaurus* could run at least as fast.

Long-frilled ceratopsians

The frill of long-frilled ceratopsians extended back to, or over, the shoulders. Sometimes the bony frill was armed with short spikes, and there were often holes in the frill to lighten the load. The snout had a short horn, and there were long brow horns – the opposite of the short-frilled ceratopsians.

Brow horn

Horn was made of solid bone

FOSSIL HORN
This fossil is the core of the brow horn of *Triceratops*. In life it would have been sheathed in horn.

IDEAL SKULL
Triceratops had a solid bony frill, a short nose horn, and two 3-ft-long (1 m) brow horns. The parrotlike beak and scissorlike teeth were ideal for *Triceratops'* vegetarian diet.

Beak was used to crop vegetation

Sharp teeth cut up leaves

TOROSAURUS
The skull of *Torosaurus*, from the tip of the snout to the back of the frill, was 8½ ft (2.6 m) long – about the size of a small car. *Torosaurus'* head was bigger than that of any other known land animal.

Two large holes in the frill bone reduced its weight.

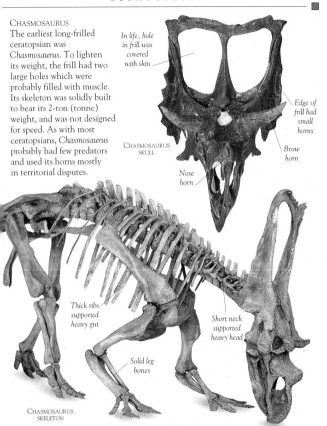

CHASMOSAURUS

The earliest long-frilled ceratopsian was *Chasmosaurus*. To lighten its weight, the frill had two large holes which were probably filled with muscle. Its skeleton was solidly built to bear its 2-ton (tonne) weight, and was not designed for speed. As with most ceratopsians, *Chasmosaurus* probably had few predators and used its horns mostly in territorial disputes.

In life, hole in frill was covered with skin

Edge of frill had small horns

Brow horn

CHASMOSAURUS SKULL

Nose horn

Thick ribs supported heavy gut

Short neck supported heavy head

Solid leg bones

CHASMOSAURUS SKELETON

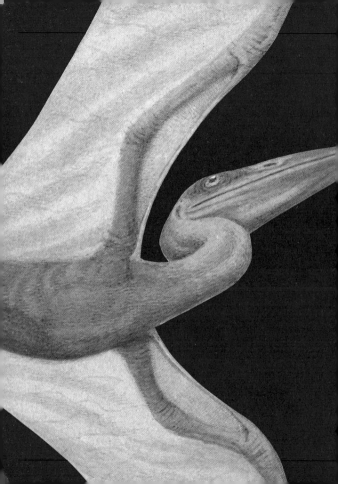

REPTILES OF THE SEA AND AIR

ABOUT SEA AND AIR REPTILES

WHILE THE DINOSAURS lived on land, other reptiles lived in the sea and flew in the air. The sea reptiles, such as the ichthyosaurs and plesiosaurs, needed to breathe air and would have surfaced frequently to fill their lungs. The flying reptiles, called pterosaurs, included the largest ever flying animals. There were two groups of pterosaur – rhamphorhynchoids and pterodactyloids.

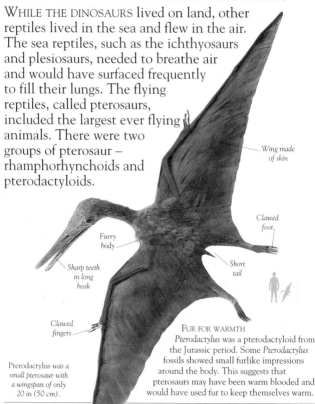

Wing made of skin

Clawed foot

Furry body

Short tail

Sharp teeth in long beak

Clawed fingers

Pterodactylus was a small pterosaur with a wingspan of only 20 in (50 cm).

FUR FOR WARMTH
Pterodactylus was a pterodactyloid from the Jurassic period. Some *Pterodactylus* fossils showed small furlike impressions around the body. This suggests that pterosaurs may have been warm blooded and would have used fur to keep themselves warm.

Tapered tail

Long skull

Large flipper

PELONEUSTES
Fish, shellfish, and smaller sea reptiles formed the diet of the sea predator *Peloneustes*. Its barrel-shaped body had large flippers for speeding through the water.

ICHTHYOSAURUS
Ichthyosaurs, such as *Ichthyosaurus*, were similar in shape to modern dolphins. Like dolphins, ichthyosaurs would have been fast swimmers due to their stream-lined shape.

Dolphins are the acrobats of the sea.

DOLPHINS
Dolphins steer with their fins as they chase fish at speeds of up to 31 mph (50 km/h). It is possible that ichthyosaurs swam as fast as dolphins, and lived in a similar manner.

Dolphins are mammals, but they have no hair.

RARE FOSSILS
Pterosaur fossils are rare because they had light, fragile bones. The lightness of the bones was important to allow flight.

Ichthyosaurus was about 6½ ft (2 m) long.

REPTILES AT SEA

THE SEA REPTILES evolved from land reptiles that adapted to life in the water. The legs and feet shortened and widened to become paddles, and the body became streamlined for faster movement through water. These reptiles were carnivores, preying on other sea creatures as well as each other.

MODIFIED PADDLE
The plesiosaur *Cryptoclidus* was 13 ft (4 m) long and had four paddles that were each about 3 ft (1 m) long. It swam by flexing these powerful paddles up and down, "flying" through the water in the way that penguins do today.

Each paddle had five elongated toes.

Large and sharp teeth

Curved and conical teeth

FLEXIBLE JAWS
Mosasaurus was a giant marine lizard that lived in Late Cretaceous shallow coastal waters. The skull and lower jaw bones had flexible joints and curved, piercing teeth. This would enable *Mosasaurus* to give a wide and lethal bite.

Powerful, flexible paddles propelled Pliosaurus through the water.

All plesiosaurs had very long necks and small heads.

PHOTOGRAPH TAKEN AT LOCH NESS.

Could this be the Loch Ness Monster?

MYSTERIOUS MONSTER

Many people claim to have seen a large creature swimming in Loch Ness in Scotland. This animal, known as the Loch Ness Monster, has been described as a living relative of the plesiosaurs.

MURAENOSAURUS

Air-filled lungs meant that the plesiosaur *Muraenosaurus* would have found it easier to float than to dive underwater. To combat this, it probably swallowed pebbles to weigh itself down, the way that crocodiles do today.

Scaly skin

Tail flipper

The skin would have been scaly, like the reptiles on land.

PLIOSAURUS

One of the fiercest predators of its time, *Pliosaurus* hunted in the seas of the Jurassic period 150 million years ago. It was about 23 ft (7 m) long and fed on fish and smaller sea reptiles. Like all pliosaurs, *Pliosaurus* had a short neck, a large head, and a barrel-shaped body. It also had strong jaws and large, sharp teeth with which it could crush and kill prey.

SEA REPTILE FACTS

• They breathed air.

• Most were carnivores.

• *Mosasaurus* swam by thrashing its tail back and forth.

• Marine iguanas, sea snakes, and turtles are modern marine reptiles.

More reptiles at sea

Plesiosaurs, pliosaurs, and turtles probably hauled themselves onto beaches to lay eggs, the way modern turtles do. Ichthyosaurs did not leave the water since they were fully adapted to life at sea and gave birth to live young. By the time the dinosaurs died out, all sea reptiles, apart from the turtles, had become extinct, too. The reason for this is as mysterious as the disappearance of the dinosaurs.

Fossil shell of the 12-in-long (30 cm) turtle Cimochelys

FOSSIL SHELLS
Fossilized ancient turtle shells show that these turtles had the same bony armor as modern turtles.

Archelon was 20 ft (6 m) long.

ARCHELON
Like its descendants, the modern turtles, *Archelon* may have returned to the same beaches every year to lay eggs. Both the adult *Archelon* and its eggs would have been vulnerable to predatory dinosaurs of that time.

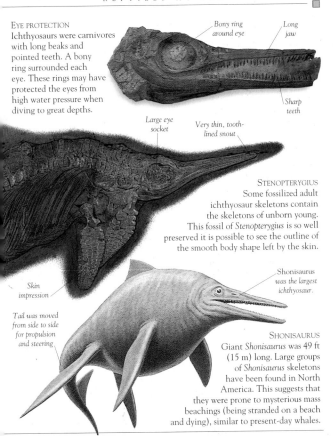

EYE PROTECTION
Ichthyosaurs were carnivores with long beaks and pointed teeth. A bony ring surrounded each eye. These rings may have protected the eyes from high water pressure when diving to great depths.

Bony ring around eye

Long jaw

Sharp teeth

Large eye socket

Very thin, tooth-lined snout

STENOPTERYGIUS
Some fossilized adult ichthyosaur skeletons contain the skeletons of unborn young. This fossil of *Stenopterygius* is so well preserved it is possible to see the outline of the smooth body shape left by the skin.

Skin impression

Tail was moved from side to side for propulsion and steering

Shonisaurus was the largest ichthyosaur.

SHONISAURUS
Giant *Shonisaurus* was 49 ft (15 m) long. Large groups of *Shonisaurus* skeletons have been found in North America. This suggests that they were prone to mysterious mass beachings (being stranded on a beach and dying), similar to present-day whales.

REPTILES IN THE AIR

THE PTEROSAURS were the first vertebrates (animals with a backbone) to use powered flight. Their wings were a thin membrane of muscles and elastic fibers covered with skin. The rhamphorhynchoid group of pterosaurs had long tails and short heads with sharp teeth. They first appeared in the Triassic period and became extinct at the end of the Jurassic period.

Stiff tail may have been used for steering when flying

RHAMPHORHYNCHUS
Rhamphorhynchus, a rhamphorhynchoid, had a special beak for trawling the water surface to catch fish while flying. The jaws were armed with large, forward-pointing spike teeth behind a toothless beak.

Large skull

Long tail typical of rhamphorhynchoids

Pointed teeth

FOSSIL
This fossil skeleton of the rhamphorhynchoid *Dimorphodon* shows the fine bones and the skull which was very large compared to the body.

EARL DOUGLASS (1862-1931) was an American from Utah. He worked at the Carnegie Museum in Pittsburgh.

WHAT HE DISCOVERED

In 1909 Douglass was sent by Andrew Carnegie to hunt for fossils in Utah. Douglass' discoveries included *Diplodocus* and *Apatosaurus*. The site where these dinosaurs were found was turned into the Dinosaur National Park, which still exists today.

BARNUM BROWN (1873-1963), an American, was hired by the American Museum of Natural History in New York because of his skill in finding dinosaur skeletons.

WHAT HE DISCOVERED

Barnum Brown's expertise in fossil hunting earned him the nickname "Mr. Bones." He found the first *Tyrannosaurus rex* fossils, and named *Ankylosaurus* and *Corythosaurus*. The AMNH houses the world's greatest display of Cretaceous dinosaurs as a result of Brown's collecting.

JIM JENSEN (1910-98) was a self-taught paleontologist. He was the curator of the Vertebrate Paleontology Research Laboratory at Brigham Young University in Provo, Utah.

WHAT HE DISCOVERED

Jensen discovered some of the largest dinosaurs. In 1972, he found a partial skeleton of a sauropod. He named it *Supersaurus*. Its height is estimated to be 54 ft (16.5 m). In 1979 he found a partial skeleton of another new sauropod. Now called *Ultrasauros*, it may be a particularly big specimen of *Brachiosaurus*.

BILL WALKER (b. 1928) is a British quarry-worker who is also an amateur fossil collector. In 1982, he made an important dinosaur discovery when exploring a muddy clay pit in Surrey, England.

WHAT HE DISCOVERED

Walker found a huge claw, which broke into pieces when he held it. He took it to the British Museum in London, which organized an excavation to recover more of the creature. It turned out to be a new dinosaur, which was named *Baryonyx walkeri*, in honor of Walker.

REPTILES CLASSIFIED

ALL LIVING THINGS are classified
into different groups, according
to their common features. In the
animal kingdom, vertebrates
form a huge group. All
vertebrates have a backbone –
that is their
common feature.
This chart shows
how reptiles,
including the
dinosaurs, fit
into the
vertebrate group.

FISH

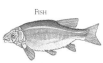

FISHES AND
SHARKS

AMPHIBIANS

AMPHIB

REPTILES

VERTEBRATES

VERTEBRATES
All vertebrates have
an internal skeleton,
which supports their
body. This distinguishes
them from animals
without an internal
skeleton, such as
insects, which are
called invertebrates.

MAMMALS

MAMMAL

FOUR GROUPS
There are four main
groups of vertebrates –
fishes, amphibians,
reptiles, and mammals.
Each of these groups
have hundreds, or even
thousands, of subgroups.

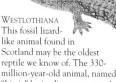

RECONSTRUCTION
OF "LIZZIE"

WESTLOTHIANA
This fossil lizard-
like animal found in
Scotland may be the oldest
reptile we know of. The 330-
million-year-old animal, named
"Lizzie" by its discoverer, was 1 ft (30 cm)
long. Although it may have been a reptile, it could also
have been an amphibian, or something in between.

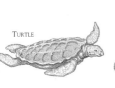

TURTLE

SNAKE

CROCODILE

Turtles

Lizards
Snakes

Thecodonts
Crocodiles

ANAPSIDS

LEPIDOSAUROMORPHS

ARCHOSAURIA

DIAPSIDS

ARCHOSAUROMORPHS

DINOSAURIA

SYNAPSIDS

EURYAPSIDS

DINOSAUR

Mammal-like
reptiles

Plesiosaurs
Ichthyosaurs

REPTILE GROUPS
The reptile group is
divided into three
subgroups. These three
divisions are based on
the number of openings
in the skull behind the
eye sockets. The
anapsids have no
openings; the synapsids
have one, and the
diapsids have two.

DIAPSIDS
The diapsids are further
divided into three
groups. These are:
lepidosauromorphs,
which include lizards
and snakes; archosauro-
morphs, which include
dinosaurs and crocodiles;
and eurapsids, which
include the plesiosaurs
and the ichthyosaurs.

ARCHOSAUROMORPHS
The dinosaurs are in
this group, as well as
the thecodonts, which
are thought to be the
ancestors of the
dinosaurs. Other
members of the
archosauromorph
group include
pterosaurs, crocodiles,
and birds.

Dinosaurs classified

The classification of dinosaurs is controversial and is continually being revised. In this chart, dinosaurs are subdivided into three main groups – Herrerasauria (early predatory dinosaurs), Saurischia, and Ornithischia. Birds (Aves) are now considered to be dinosaurs because primitive birds, such as *Archaeopteryx*, shared many features in common with theropods.

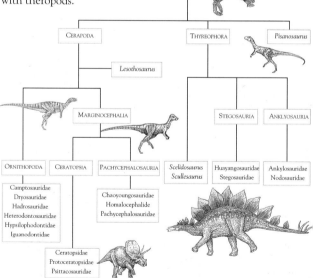

ORNITHISCHIA

CERAPODA

Lesothosaurus

THYREOPHORA

Pisanosaurus

MARGINOCEPHALIA

STEGOSAURIA

ANKLYOSAURIA

| ORNITHOPODA | CERATOPSIA | PACHYCEPHALOSAURIA | *Scelidosaurus* *Scullesaurus* | STEGOSAURIA | ANKLYOSAURIA |

ORNITHOPODA

Camptosauridae
Dryosauridae
Hadrosauridae
Heterodontosauridae
Hypsilophodontidae
Iguanodontidae

CERATOPSIA

PACHYCEPHALOSAURIA

Chaoyoungosauridae
Homalocephalide
Pachycephalosauridae

Scelidosaurus
Scullesaurus

Huayangosauridae
Stegosauridae

Ankylosauridae
Nodosauridae

Ceratopsidae
Protoceratopsidae
Psittacosauridae

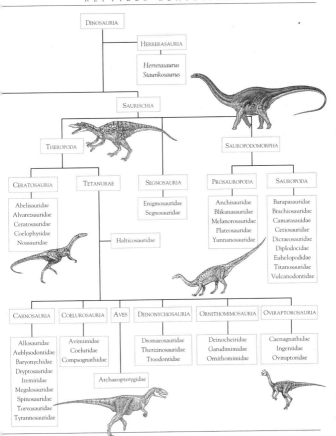

DINOSAURIA

HERRERASAURIA

Herrerasaurus
Staurikosaurus

SAURISCHIA

THEROPODA

SAUROPODOMORPHA

CERATOSAURIA

Abelisauridae
Alvarezsauridae
Ceratosauridae
Coelophysidae
Noasauridae

TETANURAE

Halticosauridae

SEGNOSAURIA

Enigmosauridae
Segnosauridae

PROSAUROPODA

Anchisauridae
Blikanasauridae
Melanorosauridae
Plateosauridae
Yunnanosauridae

SAUROPODA

Barapasauridae
Brachiosauridae
Camarasauridae
Cetiosauridae
Dicraeosauridae
Diplodocidae
Euhelopodidae
Titanosauridae
Vulcanodontidae

CARNOSAURIA

Allosauridae
Aublysodontidae
Baryonychidae
Dryptosauridae
Itemiridae
Megalosauridae
Spinosauridae
Torvosauridae
Tyrannosauridae

COELUROSAURIA

Avimimidae
Coeluridae
Compsognathidae

AVES

Archaeopterygidae

DEINONYCHOSAURIA

Dromaeosauridae
Therizinosauridae
Troodontidae

ORNITHOMIMOSAURIA

Deinocheiridae
Garudimimidae
Ornithomimidae

OVIRAPTOROSAURIA

Caenagnathidae
Ingeniidae
Oviraptoridae

RECORDS AND MYTHS

AS SCIENCE HAS ADVANCED, so has our understanding of dinosaurs. With almost every new discovery, we learn more about these giant reptiles. The early dinosaur experts had beliefs about dinosaurs which we now know to be incorrect. The largest, smallest, fastest, most intelligent, or the least intelligent dinosaur also changes as our knowledge increases.

DINOSAUR RECORDS

• The smallest dinosaur ever found was called *Mussaurus*. It was only 8 in (20 cm) long, but the single skeleton found may have been a hatchling. The smallest adult dinosaur we know of was *Compsognathus*, which was about the size of a chicken.

• *Dromiceiomimus* may have been the fastest of the dinosaurs, running at speeds of over 43 mph (70 km/h).

• The sauropod *Mamenchisaurus* had the longest neck of any dinosaur. The length of the neck was around 46 ft (14 m).

• *Carcharodontosaurus* and *Giganotosaurus* are the largest meat-eating dinosaurs discovered to date. Both dinosaurs were about 50 ft (15 m) long.

• The biggest dinosaur that we currently know of was the sauropod *Argentinoisaurus* from South America. It probably weighed about 110 tons (100 tonnes).

• The herbivorous hadrosaurs had about 960 teeth – more than any other dinosaurs. That was about 480 tightly packed teeth in each jaw.

• *Troodon* had the largest brain in proportion to its size of any dinosaur.

• *Stegosaurus* had the smallest brain in proportion to its size.

• *Diplodocus* had the longest tail of all the dinosaurs, at over 43 ft (13 m) in length.

DINOSAUR MYTHS

• In 1822, Gideon Mantell made a reconstruction of *Iguanodon*, based on the few bones he had found. He had only one thumb spike, which he thought belonged on *Iguanodon*'s nose. This was similar to the nose spike of an iguana, after which *Iguanodon* was named. It was not until the discovery of several skeletons in the late 1800s that scientists realized this mistake.

• In China, the word "konglong" means both "dinosaur" and "terrible dragon." The Chinese have been collecting dinosaur fossils for 2,000 years. Since the third century A.D., and perhaps before then, the Chinese believed that dinosaur bones were actually the remains of dragons.

• Many films and books portray dinosaurs and humans as living at the same time. In fact, dinosaurs became extinct over 60 million years before the first humans appeared.

• It used to be thought that all dinosaurs dragged their tails on the ground, like modern lizards. Some sauropods probably did, but most dinosaurs had stiffened tails, which they held horizontally off the ground.

• *Hypsilophodon* was once thought to have lived in trees. It was believed that their long tails helped them to balance in the branches, and their sharp claws were used for clinging. We now know their fingers and toes were not designed for gripping branches.

• Many people think that dinosaurs were all huge and cumbersome. But the vast majority were only about as big as an elephant, and some were as small as a chicken. Most were very agile, too.

• It was thought that *Brachiosaurus* lived in water because of the high position of its nostrils. But the great water pressures at depth would not have allowed it to breathe.

• *Iguanodon* was the first dinosaur to be reconstructed. At first it was shown as a slow, sprawling lizard, dragging a fat belly on the ground. We now know that *Iguanodon* was actually bipedal and much slimmer.

DIGGING UP DINOSAURS

MANY IMPORTANT dinosaur discoveries are made by professional and amateur collectors. Once discovered, fossil bones should be removed only by experienced professionals, because the bones are often fragile. The method of removing the bones depends on a number of factors, but generally follows a similar procedure.

1 SITE
Once a dinosaur site has been uncovered, the fossil bones have to be excavated (dug up). This delicate operation is carried out using special tools.

3 EXPOSING THE BONES
Whenever possible, the matrix is removed close to the bone. This is done with great care so as to not damage the bone. The bones are exposed to reveal their full size so that no fragment will be left behind when removed.

2 EXCAVATION
Hammers, chisels, and picks are used to remove most of the matrix (earth and stone material surrounding the bones).

5 JACKET ON OTHER SIDE
Once the exposed part of the bone has been coated, the rest of the bone, including some of the matrix, can be dug out of the ground. It is then covered with a plaster and burlap jacket.

4 PLASTER JACKET
The exposed part of the bones are coated with glue and covered with a jacket of plaster and burlap (a type of canvas). This will protect the bones as they travel from the site to a museum, where they can be studied in more detail.

6 REMOVAL FROM SITE
The jacketed bones are sometimes so big and heavy that a crane is needed to lift them onto a truck.

Resources

USA

Academy of Natural Sciences of Philadelphia
1900 Benjamin Franklin Parkway
Philadelphia, PA 19103

American Museum of Natural History
Central Park West
at 79th Street
New York, NY 10024

Buffalo Museum of Science
1020 Humboldt Parkway
Buffalo, NY 14211

Carnegie Museum of Natural History
4400 Forbes Avenue
Pittsburgh, PA 15213

Cleveland Museum of Natural History
Wade Oval Drive
University Circle
Cleveland, OH 44106

Denver Museum of Natural History
2001 Colorado Boulevard
Denver, CO 80205

Dinosaur National Monument
4545 E. Highway 40
Dinosaur, CO 81610

Earth Science Museum
Brigham Young University
1683 North Canyon Road
Provo, UT 84602

Exhibit Museum of Natural History
University of Michigan
1109 Geddes Avenue
Ann Arbor, MI 48109

Field Museum of Natural History
1400 S. Lake Shore Drive
Chicago, IL 60605

Fort Worth Museum of Science and History
1501 Montgomery Street
Forth Worth, TX 76107

Geological Museum
P.O. Box 3006
S.H. Knight Geology Building
University of Wyoming
Laramie, WY 82071

Houston Museum of Natural Science
1 Hermann Circle Drive
Houston, TX 77030

Museum of Comparative Zoology
26 Oxford Street
Harvard University
Cambridge, MA 02138

Museum of Northern Arizona
3101 N. Fort Valley Road
Flagstaff, AZ 86001

Museum of Paleontology
University of California
1101 Valley Life Sciences Building
Berkeley, CA 94720

Museum of the Rockies
Montana State University
600 W. kagy Blvd.
Bozeman, MT 59717

National Museum of Natural History
10th Street and Constitution Ave. NW
Smithsonian Institution
Washington, D.C. 20560

Natural History Museum of Los Angeles County
900 Exposition Boulevard
Los Angeles, CA 90007

Peabody Museum of Natural History
Yale University
170 Whitney Avenue
New Haven, CT 06520

Pratt Museum of Natural History
Amherst College
Amherst, MA 01002

Utah Museum of Natural History
1390 E. President's Circle
University of Utah
Salt Lake City, UT 84112

CANADA

Calgary Zoo, Botanical Garden and Prehistoric Park
1300 Zoo Road NE
Calgary, AB T2M 4R8

Canadian Museum of Nature
Victoria Memorial Museum Building
240 McLeod Avenue
Ottawa, ONT K1A 0M8

Dinosaur Provincial Park
P.O. Box 60
Patricia AB P0J 2K0

Museum of Natural Sciences
University of Saskatchewan
Department of Geological Sciences
114 Science Place
Saskatoon SK S7N 0W0

The Manitoba Museum
190 Rupert Avenue
Winnipeg MB R3B 0N2

Nova Scotia Museum of Natural History
1747 Summer Street
Halifax NS B3H 3A6

Provincial Museum of Alberta
12845 102nd Avenue
Edmonton AB T5N 0M6

Redpath Museum
McGill University
859 Sherbrook Street West
Montreal QC H3A 2K6

Royal Ontario Museum
100 Queen's Park
Toronto ON M5S 2C6

Royal Saskatchewan Museum
2445 Albert Square
Regina SK S4P 3Z7

Tyrrell Museum of Palaeontology
Highway 838
Midland Provincial Park
Drumheller AB T0J 0Y0

Pronunciation guide

ALBERTOSAURUS
(al-BERT-oh-SORE-us)

ALLOSAURUS
(al-oh-SORE-us)

ANCHISAURUS
(AN-ki-SORE-us)

ANKYLOSAURUS
(an-KIE-loh-SORE-us)

APATOSAURUS
(ah-PAT-oh-SORE-us)

ARCHAEOPTERYX
(ark-ee-OP-ter-iks)

BAROSAURUS
(bar-oh-SORE-us)

BARYONYX
(bar-ee-ON-iks)

BRACHIOSAURUS
(brak-ee-oh-SORE-us)

CARNOTAURUS
(kar-noh-TOR-us)

CENTROSAURUS
(SEN-troh-SORE-us)

CERATOSAURUS
(seh-rat-oh-SORE-us)

CETIOSAURUS
(see-tee-oh-SORE-us)

CHASMOSAURUS
(kaz-moh-SORE-us)

COELOPHYSIS
(SEEL-oh-FIE-sis)

COMPSOGNATHUS
(komp-soh-NAY-thus)

CORYTHOSAURUS
(koh-rith-oh-SORE-us)

CRIORHYNCHUS
(cry-oh-RINK-us)

CRYPTOCLIDUS
(cript-oh-CLIE-dus)

DASPLETOSAURUS
(das-PLEE-toh-SORE-us)

DEINOCHEIRUS
(DINE-oh-KEE-rus)

DEINONYCHUS
(die-NON-i-kus)

DIMORPHODON
(die-MORF-oh-don)

DIPLODOCUS
(di-PLOH-de-kus)

DROMAEOSAURUS
(DROH-may-oh-SORE-us)

DROMICEIOMIMUS
(droh-MEE-see-oh-MEEM-us)

EDMONTONIA
(ed-mon-TONE-ee-ah)

EDMONTOSAURUS
(ed-MON-toh-SORE-us)

EORAPTOR
(EE-oh-RAP-tor)

EUOPLOCEPHALUS
(you-op-loh-SEF-ah-lus)

EUSTREPTOSPONDYLUS
(yoo-STREP-toh-SPON-die-lus)

GALLIMIMUS
(gal-lee-MEEM-us)

GRYPOSAURUS
(GRIPE-oh-SORE-us)

HADROSAURUS
(HAD-roh-SORE-us)

HERRERASAURUS
(eh-ray-rah-SORE-us)

HETERODONTOSAURUS
(HET-er-oh-DONT-oh-SORE-us)

HYPACROSAURUS
(high-PAK-roh-SORE-us)

HYPSILOPHODON
(hip-sih-LOH-foh-don)

ICTHYOSAURUS
(IKH-thee-oh-SORE-us)

IGUANODON
(ig-WHA-noh-don)

INGENIA
(in-GAY-nee-a)

KENTROSAURUS
(KEN-troh-SORE-us)

LAMBEOSAURUS
(LAMB-ee-oh-SORE-us)

MAIASAURA
(MY-ah-SORE-ah)

MAMENCHISAURUS
(mah-MEN-chee-SORE-us)

MASOSAURUS
(MAZ-oh-SORE-us)

MASSOSPONDYLUS
(MAS-oh-SPON-die-lus)

MEGALOSAURUS
(MEG-ah-loh-SORE-us)

MELANOROSAURUS
(MEL-an-or-oh-SORE-us)

MURAENOSAURUS
(mure-rain-oh-SORE-us)

MUSSAURUS
(mus-OR-us)

MUTTABURRASAURUS
(MUT-a-BUR-a-SORE-us)

ORNITHOLESTES
(OR-nith-OH-LES-teez)

ORNITHOMIMUS
(OR-ni-thoh-MEE-mus)

OURANOSAURUS
(OO-ran-oh-SORE-us)

OVIRAPTOR
(OHV-ih-RAP-tor)

PACYCEPHALOSAURUS
(PAK-ee-SEF-a-loh-SORE-US)

PARASAUROLOPHUS
(par-a-SORE-oh-LOAF-us)

PELONEUSTES
(pel-oh-nee-OOST-ees)

PINACOSAURUS
(pin-AK-oh-SORE-us)

PLATEOSAURUS
(PLAT-ee-oh-SORE-us)

PLIOSAURUS
(plie-oh-SORE-us)

POLACANTHUS
(pol-a-KAN-thus)

PRENOCEPHALE
(pren-oh-SEF-a-lee)

PSITTACOSAURUS
(Si-tak-oh-SORE-us)

PTERANODON
(teh-RANN-oh-don)

PTERODACTYLUS
(teh-roh-DACT-illus)

QUETZALCOATLUS
(kwet-zal-COAT-lus)

RHAMPHORHYNCHUS
(RAM-foh-RING-khus)

RIOJASAURUS
(ree-O-ha-SORE-us)

SALTASAURUS
(sal-te-SORE-us)

SAUROPELTA
(SORE-oh-PEL-ta)

SEISMOSAURUS
(SIZE-moh-SORE-us)

SHONISAURUS
(shon-ee-SORE-us)

SORDES
(SOHR-deez)

STEGOCERAS
(ste-GOS-er-as)

STEGOSAURUS
(STEG-oh-SORE-us)

STENOPTERYGIUS
(sten-OP-teh-RIDGE-ee-us)

STRUTHIOMIMUS
(STRUTH-ee-oh-MEEM-us)

STYGIMOLOCH
(STIJ-i-MOH-lok)

STYRACOSAURUS
(sty-RAK-oh-SORE-us)

SUPERSAURUS
(SUE-per-SORE-us)

TOROSAURUS
(tor-oh-SORE-us)

TRICERATOPS
(try-SERRA-tops)

TROODON
(TROH-oh-don)

TUOJIANGOSAURUS
(toh-HWANG-oh-SORE-us)

TYRANNOSAURUS
(tie-RAN-oh-SORE-us)

ULTRASAURUS
(ul-tra-SORE-us)

VELOCIRAPTOR
(vel-O-si-RAP-tor)

Glossary

AMPHIBIANS
A group of animals that are able to live both on land and in water.

ANKYLOSAURS
Quadrupedal, armored ornithischians.

ARMORED DINOSAURS
Dinosaurs whose bodies were protected by bony plates or spikes. These included ankylosaurs and some sauropods.

ARCHOSAUROMORPHS
A major group of reptiles which includes dinosaurs, thecodonts, pterosaurs, crocodiles, and birds.

BIPEDAL
Walking on the two hind legs only.

CARNIVORE
An animal that eats meat.

CARNOSAURS
A group of large theropods.

CERATOPSIANS
Quadrupedal ornithischians. Most ceratopsians had heads decorated with horns and frills.

CLASSIFICATION
The process of arranging animals into groups, related by common physical features.

COLD-BLOODED
Dependent on conditions outside the body for temperature regulation, such as the Sun's heat, to give warmth to the body.

CONIFERS
Trees that bear cones, such as pines and firs.

CONTINENTAL DRIFT
The constant movement of the plates which make up the Earth's lithosphere.

CRETACEOUS PERIOD
The third period of the Mezozoic era – 65-145 million years ago.

DIAPSID
A reptile group which includes the archosauromorphs, the lepidosauromorphs, and the euryapsids.

DINOSAURS
An extinct group of archosauromorphs with an erect stance. They

included the ancestors of modern birds.

EURYAPSIDS
A reptile group which includes the two groups of sea reptiles: plesiosaurs and ichthyosaurs.

EXTINCTION
The process by which living things die out of existence.

FOSSIL
The preserved remains of something that once lived.

GASTROLITHS
Stones that are swallowed to help grind up food in the stomach.

HADROSAURS
Large ornithopods with ducklike bills, of which there were two groups: lambeosaurines and hadrosaurines.

HERBIVORE
An animal that feeds on plants.

INVERTEBRATES
Animals without a backbone.

ISCHIUM
One of the two lower

hipbones of dinosaurs (the other was the pubis). The ischium anchored muscles that worked the hind legs.

JURASSIC PERIOD
The second period of the Mesozoic era – 145-208 million years ago.

LITHOSPHERE
The Earth's crust and upper mantle. It is approximately 124 miles (200 km) thick.

MESOZOIC ERA
The period of time between 65-245 million years ago. The Mesozoic era incorporated the Triassic, Jurassic, and Cretaceous periods.

ORNITHISCHIANS
The "bird-hipped" dinosaurs. One of the two major groups of dinosaurs.

ORNITHOPODS
Small to very large plant-eating ornithischians that were mostly bipedal.

PACHYCEPHALOSAURS
Bipedal ornithopods. Also known as bone-headed dinosaurs, because the roof of their skull was very thick.

PALEONTOLOGIST
A person who studies fossils.

PROSAUROPODS
Small to large early sauropodomorphs.

PTEROSAURS
The flying reptiles of the Mesozoic era. Distant cousins of the dinosaurs.

PUBIS
One of the two lower hipbones of dinosaurs (the other was the ischium). In some dinosaurs, the pubis anchored the muscle that pulled the hind legs forward.

QUADRUPEDAL
Walking on all four legs.

REPTILES
A group of "cold-blooded" vertebrates with scaly skin.

SAURISCHIANS
The "lizard-hipped" dinosaurs. One of the two major groups of dinosaurs.

SAUROPODOMORPHS
A group of quadrupedal herbivorous dinosaurs with long tails and necks. This group included the largest land animals that ever lived.

SAUROPODS
Large to immense sauropodomorphs.

STEGOSAURS
Quadrupedal ornithischians with two rows of plates and/or spines running along the neck, back, and tail.

SYNAPSIDS
A reptile group that includes mammallike reptiles (they are distantly related to mammals).

THECODONTS
A group of archosauromorphs which are the ancestors of the dinosaurs.

THEROPODS
Bipedal, carnivorous saurischian dinosaurs.

TRIASSIC PERIOD
The first period of the Mesozoic era – 208-245 million years ago.

VERTEBRAE
Bones of the spinal column.

VERTEBRATES
Animals with backbones.

WARM-BLOODED
Maintaining body warmth by turning the energy gained by food into heat.

Index

Acknowledgments

Dorling Kindersley would like to thank:

Hilary Bird for the index. Camela Decaire, Ray Rogers, Esther Labi and Robert Graham and Darren Tankefor editorial assistance. Carnegie Museum of Natural History for use of *Apatosaurus* skeleton on pages 90/91. Louis Rey for the *Velociraptor* model on p. 55cl and 81b.

Photographs by:

Paul Bricknell, Andy Crawford, John Douns, Lynton Gardiner, Steve Gorton, Colin Keates, Gary Kevin, Dave King, William Lindsay, Ray Moller, Miguel Periera, Tim Ridley, Dave Rudlan, Bruce Selyen, Paul Sereno, Harry Taylor, Jerry Young

Illustrations by:

Roby Braun, Lynn Chadwick, Simone End, Eugene Fleury, Giuliano Fornari, Steve Kirk, Janos Marffy, Ikkyu Murakawa, Andrew Robinson, Graham Rosewarne, John Sibbick, John Temperton, John Woodcock.

Picture credits: t = top b = bottom c = center l= left r = right
American Museum of Natural History 140tl; 141 cl, Roby Braun 66tr.

Dougal Dixon 53b.
Fortean 126tl.
Frank Lane Picture Library/Eric and David Hosking 55tr.
Hulton Picture Library 18tl; 138tl.
Image Bank/Robert Hardrie 135tl.
Kobal 23tl. Ikkyu Murakawa 114cl; 114cr.
Museum of the Rockies/Bruce Selyem 57tr; 76 77c; 150tl; 150bl; 150r; 151l; 151tr; 151br.
Natural History Museum, London 23br 102cr; 105tl; 136.
Science Photo Library/Julian Baum 134 bl. John Sereno 58tr. John Sibbick 55br; 106bl.

Every effort has been made to trace the copyright holders and we apologize in advance for any unintentional omissions. We would be pleased to insert the appropriate acknowledgment in any subsequent edition of this publication.

All other images © Dorling Kindersley
For further information see:
www.dkimages.com